Saint & Greavsie's
WORLD
CUP
SPECIAL

A MATCH-BY-MATCH DIARY OF ALL THE MATCHES AND MOST MEMORABLE MOMENTS OF ITALIA '90

Ian St John and Jimmy Greaves
Edited by Norman Giller

Stanley Paul
London   Sydney   Auckland   Johannesburg

Stanley Paul & Co. Ltd

An imprint of the Random Century Group
20 Vauxhall Bridge Road, London SW1V 2SA

Random Century Australia (Pty) Ltd
20 Alfred Street, Milsons Point, Sydney,
NSW 2061

Random Century New Zealand Limited
191 Archers Road, PO Box 40-086, Glenfield,
Auckland 10

Century Hutchinson South Africa Ltd
PO Box 337, Bergvlei 2012, South Africa

First published 1990

Set in 10pt Century Schoolbook
and designed by Norman Giller Enterprises
Westcliff-on-Sea, Essex

Printed and bound in Great Britain
by Scotprint Ltd, Musselburgh, Scotland

**British Library Cataloguing
in Publication Data**

St John, Ian 1938-
Saint & Greavsie's World Cup Special.
1. Association football. Competitions. World Cup
I. Title II. Greaves, Jimmy 1940- III. Giller,
Norman 1940-
796.334668

ISBN 0 09 174629 9

Acknowledgements

The authors and publishers would like to thank
the following for use of copyright photographs:

Bob Thomas Sports Photography
AllSport
Colorsport
Action Images
Empics

Thanks also to Robin Bouttell for his jacket
drawing, and to Barry Roberts for the 'Saint and
Greavsie Time Machine' cartoon strip; and to
Michael Giller for his World Cup statistics.

Saint and Greavsie and Norman Giller would
like particularly to thank Roddy Bloomfield,
Marion Paull, Louise Speller, Graham Hart
and all the staff at Stanley Paul for their skilled
and enthusiastic help in guiding this book into
the publishing net.

Finally, thanks from Ian and Jimmy to Richard
Worth and the *Saint & Greavsie* team at LWT
for helping them to be screened and heard while
gathering material for this *World Cup Special*.

World Cup Special: Contents

Between pages 64 and 65: Saint & Greavsie's Time Machine
A Barry Roberts cartoon special

World Cup '90: Introduction

Well here we are at the start of our journey, Greavsie. By the time this book is finished we will know not only the winners of World Cup '90 but also the shape of things to come in the game. Our match-by-match diary is going to put both of us on the spot because we will be reporting the action as it happens, and you can bet we'll get caught out with a lot of contradictions.

I'm game if you are, Saint. We'll call it as we see it, and if we're made to look fools it won't be for the first or last time. I'll be first to put my head on the chopping block by predicting a victory for West Germany. Franz Beckenbauer has gone on record as saying that this is the best German squad he has ever been associated with. Kaiser Franz is normally cautious and hands out praise sparingly, so his German team must be something really special. Which team are you tipping to win the World Cup?

I'm going for Brazil. Half their team is based in Italy and they will feel comfortable with the conditions. Their manager Sebastiao Lazaroni has been experimenting with a system in which he is mixing the discipline of European football with the flair of the Brazilian game. That could prove a winning combination. What are your hopes for England?

The best I think we can expect is a place in the quarter-finals. Holland and Ireland will give us a lot of trouble in the group matches, but I believe we should manage to finish in second place

Facing page: Saint and Greavsie meet the World Cup mascot in Rome before the kick off to World Cup '90. "Here Saint," said Greavsie, "don't look now but I think the English football hooligans have already hit the stadium behind us. It's in a right old state."

ahead of Jack Charlton's Republic of Ireland. Holland should finish top of the group if Ruud Gullit and Marco van Basten can find their best form. Anything less than a place in the quarter-finals will be considered a failure for Bobby Robson, who has just astonished us on the eve of the World Cup by announcing that he will quit at the end of the tournament to take a club job with PSV Eindhoven. The timing of his resignation will not exactly help team morale. You and I, Saint, have always been supporters of Robson and I hope he makes a bold farewell because the media will be lining up to crucify him if things go wrong. He has nothing to lose now, and he just might be brave enough to give flair players like Paul Gascoigne, David Platt and Paul Parker their head. You never know, if skilful players like Chris Waddle, John Barnes and Gary Lineker all turn it on together we could have our best World Cup campaign since 1966.

What happened in 1966, Jim? Oh yes, I remember. England won the World Cup. It's not a fact that leaps immediately to the minds of we Scots. I wish I felt optimistic about Scotland's chances. We have been terrible in the build-up to the finals and our group looks like a mountain. I cannot feel confident about us beating Brazil or Sweden, and even Costa Rica give me the jitters. My prediction is a Brazil versus West Germany final, with Austria as the dark horses.

I'll go for a West Germany versus Italy final. The Italians have been looking as strong as ever in defence during their build-up matches, and in Gianluca Vialli and Robert Baggio they have two outstanding forwards with the guile to break down any defence. My outsiders are Yugoslavia. I bet we're going to look right twits before the shooting and shouting is over. Just let's hope it's a World Cup full of all the good things about the game. We'll soon see.

THE GROUPS: *Who plays where*

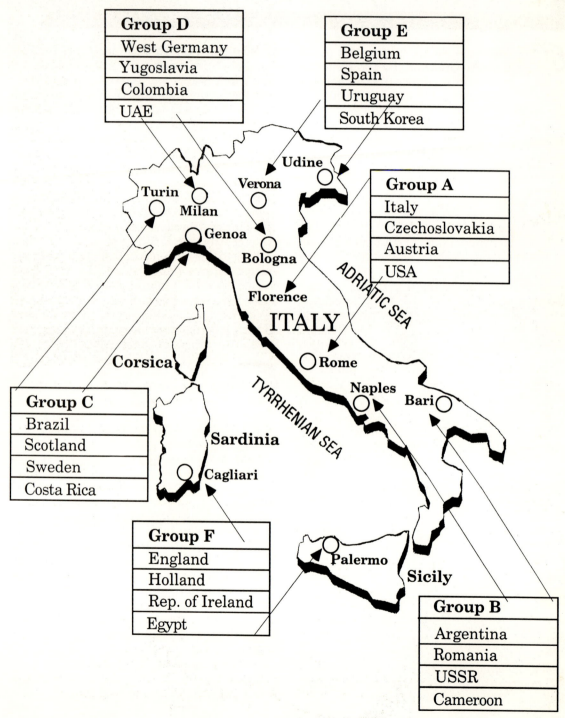

Group D
- West Germany
- Yugoslavia
- Colombia
- UAE

Group E
- Belgium
- Spain
- Uruguay
- South Korea

Group A
- Italy
- Czechoslovakia
- Austria
- USA

Group C
- Brazil
- Scotland
- Sweden
- Costa Rica

Group F
- England
- Holland
- Rep. of Ireland
- Egypt

Group B
- Argentina
- Romania
- USSR
- Cameroon

Turin

Milan

Verona

Udine

Genoa

Bologna

Florence

ITALY

ADRIATIC SEA

Corsica

Rome

TYRRHENIAN SEA

Naples

Bari

Sardinia

Cagliari

Palermo

Sicily

Greavsie reports

If you had held a nationwide competition for a forecast of the most unbelievable kick-off to World Cup '90, this result would have been dismissed as too far-fetched.

It was not just the Cameroon victory which caused a shock that could have been measured on the Richter scale. What made it even more mind-blowing was the fact that the Africans achieved their win over the reigning world champions with just nine men left on the pitch at the end of one of the most sensational games in football history.

There could not have been a better setting for this breath-taking start to the World Cup. The magnificently reconstructed and re-named San Siro stadium, where I once earned my daily bread with AC Milan, had been alive with the sound of music from La Scala opera house at the grand and colourful opening ceremony. But the Argies did not know whether they were on their arias or their elbows as Cameroon tore into them with a mix 'n' match blend of subtle skills and stark violence.

Argentina strutted around as if they had the game won before a ball had been kicked, and they paid dearly for their complacency against a team that was not in the slightest bit overawed by the challenge of kicking off the World Cup finals.

Only Diego Maradona looked the part of a world champion in a strangely lethargic Argentinian side, and the Cameroon defenders left their mark on him with tackles that were right out of the school of thuggery. This was the unacceptable face of football, but the Africans balanced their nastiness with technique and ball control that made a mockery of their rating as 500–1 outsiders.

Maradona could not even find the helping hand of God to help him shake off his markers, and he lost any chance of sympathy for his

François Omam Biyick rises to head home the first goal of World Cup '90

rough treatment by the way he over-reacted to challenges that were often more clumsy than calculated violence. Those of us who have been on the painful end of cynical tackles from Argentinian teams in the dim and distant past were quietly pleased to see them getting a taste of their own medicine.

French referee Michel Vautrot followed FIFA's ruling to stamp down on rough play to fanatical lengths, and he had collected four names before ordering off Andre Kana Biyick in the 62nd minute for what looked an accidental trip on Argentinian substitute Claudio Caniggia. Andre left the field blowing kisses to a 74,000 crowd that made no secret of their support for the underdogs.

Just four minutes later Andre's brother, François Omam Biyick, gave Cameroon the kiss of life with an astonishing goal. He met a cross from the left with a downward header which goalkeeper Nery Pumpido amazingly allowed to screw through his hands and over the line. It was a gift of a goal, but the truth is that Cameroon deserved their lead because they had been the more enterprising and industrious side from the first kick of World Cup '90. The cheers of the crowd and the delight of the billions watching on worldwide television could not have been greater had the Africans just scored the goal that won the World Cup.

Cameroon call themselves the 'Indomitable Lions', and, incredibly, Argentina had tamely surrendered to them like lambs to the slaughter. Nobody was crying for Argentina because they have won few friends with their arrogant approach to football, and I thought Maradona was lucky not to get booked as he tried to influence the referee with non-stop complaints and petulant comments.

There had been just sporadic flashes of Argentinian artistry before this stunning goal, but the fight and spirit suddenly left them like air escaping from a deflated balloon. It was Cameroon who kept battling for every ball, and they went too far with their enthusiasm in the 87th minute when Ben Massing was sent off for a flying tackle on Caniggia that would not have been out of place at Twickenham.

Cameroon finished the game with nine men and one of the sweetest and certainly most sensational victories in World Cup history. It's a funny old game!

 ## Saint comments

There could not have been a better send-off. So many World Cup finals in the past have got off to a tame start, but this victory by Cameroon meant the World Cup was bubbling with interest and excitement from the first moments.

As delighted as I was for Cameroon, I was very disappointed with Argentina's performance. They were just a shadow of the side that won the World Cup four years ago, and Maradona was too much of a prima donna for my taste. Buster Douglas prepared us for the year of the underdog with his defeat of Mike Tyson, but Cameroon topped even that!

QUOTE UNQUOTE

François Biyick, Cameroon's goal hero who plays in the French league with Stade Laval: "It was my dream to come here to Italy and score the first goal in the finals. Now that dream has come true. Perhaps people will now stop asking us questions about witch-doctors and whether we eat monkeys, and ask instead about our football."

Diego Maradona: "In some ways I am happy because I participated in making Italy non-racist. All the support today was for Cameroon. I think that was very nice. But I feel sorry for our supporters who travelled here and for those back home in Argentina. We have let them down. We are not blaming our goalkeeper. You cannot blame one player for this performance. We all lost. We never got going. We had three early chances and were punished for not taking them. We can still win the World Cup, but we have to win against the Soviet Union and Romania. It will not be easy but it can be done if our coach can find the right team formula. When Cameroon scored it hurt me as much as if my legs had been broken."

Dr Carlos Bilardo, Argentine manager who is also a renowned cancer specialist: "This is the worst thing that has ever happened to me. I do not think it is correct to call us a one-man team. Maradona is an excellent player, and it is he who sets the standards that his teammates have to try to match. What we lacked today was accuracy. We are missing our touch of class and must work at restoring it as quickly as possible. This is a bad day for us, but it is in our power to recover."

Valeri Nepomniachi, Cameroon's poker-faced Russian manager: "These things happen in football. It is what makes it such a fascinating game. We do not have time to celebrate. We must now start thinking about our next game against Romania."

Saint reports

 Greavsie reports

The new-found freedom that Romania are enjoying out of the shadow of the Ceausescu regime shone through in their opening match against the Soviet Union, who were desperately lacking a 'perestroikers' (sorry for that alleged joke out of the Greavsie school of humour).

The Italian tournament organisers generously paid for 1000 Romanian supporters to watch their country compete in the finals, and they were treated to a cracking performance by a team that was always a thought and a deed ahead of a Soviet side that never got out of first gear.

The match was virtually decided in the 15-minute spell either side of the half-time interval. Just as it looked as if the Soviets were taking command after a dodgy start, jet-heeled Romanian striker Marius Lacatus tore the heart out of them with a beautifully struck goal in the 41st minute. He outpaced his marker Valsili Rats before beating goalkeeper Rinat Dasayev at the near post with a thundering drive.

The goal gave the Romanians new belief in themselves and they started the second half with an all-out blitz. Lacatus, who formed a dynamic combination with Florin Raducioiu, put Soviet sweeper Khidiatullin under pressure and he was unlucky to handle the ball while making a desperate attempt to clear his lines. Television replays proved that the handling was just outside the box, but the Uruguayan referee pointed to the penalty spot.

Lacatus lashed the spot-kick wide of Dasayev for his and Romania's second goal that wrapped up the game.

It was too early in the tournament to leap to conclusions, but Romania looked full of daring and rich with promise.

Carlos Valderrama, the man with the orange mop on his head, justified his rating as a world-class player with a hair-raising performance against the United Arab Emirates who never looked better than second rate.

The Arabs played only to avoid defeat, hiding their goal behind a packed defence and leaving just Adnan Khamis Talyani upfield as a lonely striker. He had the best scoring chance of the first half, but seemed so surprised to find himself with an empty goal facing him that he steered his shot wide.

Colombia had a frustrating first half, dominating the play but unable to find a way through to goal against defenders who were often wild with their tackles. English referee George Courtney was one of the busiest men on the pitch, and he booked both the Meer brothers, Eisa and Ibrahim, for reckless challenges.

Colombia, with Valderrama knitting pretty patterns into their play, got the breakthrough they deserved in the 51st minute. Leonel Alvarez, who almost matched Valderrama for length of hair as well as skill, made a sudden surge down the right wing before crossing a perfect ball that Bernado Redin headed powerfully into the net.

Emirates were forced to come out of their defensive shell, and Colombia started to find gaps to exploit. They were well worth their second goal in the 87th minute. Alvarez aimed an inch-perfect pass from the half-way line into the path of Valderrama who was in full stride when he beat advancing goalkeeper Mosabah Faraj with a deadly accurate shot into the far corner of the net. It was a goal of real class and underlined the fact that Colombia would be dangerous opponents for even the most fancied teams.

Saint reports

Cameroon brought me out of my seat with excitement. Italy had me purring with pure pleasure. This was a thoroughbred performance by the host nation, and I started to want to hedge my bet that Brazil would emerge as the winners of World Cup '90.

I said to Greavsie before the match that I thought Italy might struggle to produce their best because of the enormous pressure of expectation being poured on them by their fanatical supporters. But they unveiled an exhibition of purist football that was better than anything I have seen from an Italian team in years.

Some of their passing movements could have been set to music, and all that was missing was a player able to provide the final beat. Giuseppe Giannini was the gifted conductor, and he created enough chances for the Italians to have swept to a four-or-five-goal lead before the game was an hour old.

But they were hitting and missing in front of goal, and the Austrians were still in with a chance of stealing a point despite being on the receiving end of an avalanche of attacks. The crucial moment of the match came when Andrea Carnevale was substituted after frittering away at least four golden chances. He had hardly got settled on the bench when the man who replaced him, Salvatore Schillaci, netted the vital goal in the 78th minute.

Gianluca Vialli, the most accomplished player on view, made a penetrating run deep into the right side of the overworked Austrian defence before sending a centre looping into the goalmouth where Schillaci arrived like an assassin with only one target in mind. His neck muscles bulged as he headed the ball into the net from a range of just six yards.

What was so impressive about Italy is that they outplayed an Austrian team that looked extremely competent, and able to give most teams in the tournament a torrid time. They looked almost overawed against Italy, and were lucky to escape with just a 1–0 defeat.

I could not understand why they left their leading domestic marksman, Gerhard Rodax, on the substitutes' bench. Without him they just did not have the power and the guile to break down an Italian defence in which sweeper Franco Baresi was in exceptional form.

So often in the past Italian teams have shut up shop after getting their noses in front, but I was delighted to see this side ready to express themselves as an attacking force right through to the final whistle. Manager Azeglio Vicini had the luxury of being able to leave the world's most expensive player, £8 million Roberto Baggio, on the sidelines. On the evidence of this display, it was difficult to see how a place could be found even for this master.

The crowd of 72,303 paid an unbelievable £2.1 million to watch this classic match, and I reckon even Austrian fans considered they had got excellent value for money. Football is alive and well and kicking in Italy!

Greavsie comments

Like the Saint, I thoroughly enjoyed watching Italy's performance against Austria but I was concerned by their failure to take their chances in front of goal. You could almost hear the Italian fans wishing for old heroes like a Rossi, a Riva or a Boninsegna to bang the ball into the net as they carved up the Austrian defence as easily as if it was Wiener schnitzel.

Poor old Carnevale, used to having Maradona and Careca as sidekicks at Napoli, was the biggest culprit and he must have had mixed feelings as he watched Schillaci thumping the ball into the net just moments after taking his place in the attack. The carnival had stopped for Carnevale. I was impressed by the impact Schillaci, the hit man from Sicily, made in his brief appearance. He had a touch of Steve Bull about him, not particularly elegant but a player dedicated to scoring goals. We could hear a lot more of him before the final shots of World Cup '90 have been fired.

Greavsie reports

The American dream turned into a nightmare as Czechoslovakia exposed the limitations of a United States side that was so far out of its depth that no lifebelt could have saved it.

I thought it was a good thing for the future of football in the United States when they qualified for the finals, but this defeat will have put the spreading of the "soccer is a kick in the grass" gospel back years.

The Americans were so technically and tactically naive that it was embarrassing to watch them. Czechoslovakia could easily have netted ten goals but for the fact that too many of their players were seeking personal glory rather than creating chances for team-mates.

Tomas Skuhravy scored two goals and looked a classy player but it was difficult to form a proper opinion because the opposition was so woefully weak.

It was so easy for the Czechs that they became cocky and over-confident, and they carelessly allowed Paul Caligiuri to score during a rare breakaway raid.

The Americans seemed determined to make it a doddle for the Czechs, and got one of their more accomplished players, Eric Wynalda, ordered off for a foul off the ball. Continually exposed to the perils of panic, they conceded two penalties. The first was coolly fired home by Michal Bilek, but he managed tamely to chip the second into the hands of goalkeeper Tony Meola, who must have felt as exposed as a man facing a firing squad.

Perhaps it is unfair to judge the Americans on this opening performance, but my feeling at the final whistle was that they would be buried under an avalanche of goals in their second match against the favourites Italy. The World Cup is a whole new ball game for the Americans. They've got a lot of learning to do.

Saint reports

Brazil, my tip for the Cup, made a only a fairly impressive start. It was quickly apparent that they are not overloaded with exceptional individualists as with past Brazilian sides, but their teamwork and neat passing patterns suggested they had come well prepared for a strong challenge.

The one player who looked as if he could be mentioned in the same breath as the likes of Pelé, Garrincha and Didi was Careca, who practises his art on an Italian landscape with Napoli.

He scored two superb goals, one either side of half-time, seemingly to sink a sound but unspectacular Swedish team that came into the finals with a fine defensive record that included two goalless draws with England.

Just as I was thinking that Brazil could make my World Cup winning forecast come right, they suddenly had ten mad minutes when they threatened to throw the game away. They allowed exciting youngster Tomas Brolin to turn in the box and score with a low shot in the 78th minute during a period when their defence looked decidedly shaky and unsure. The samba drums of their colourful supporters became strangely silent.

But Brazil had regained their composure and control by the end of the match and might have snatched another couple of goals in the closing moments. This restored my faith in them, and I looked forward to seeing more of the silky-smooth Careca who looked a cracker of a player. His first goal in the 40th minute was the best so far of World Cup '90. He was put clear by a stunning pass from Branco, feinted to send goalkeeper Thomas Ravelli to the right and then dragged the ball round him to the left before slotting it home. It was a piece of traditional Brazilian magic.

Greavsie reports

Before a ball had been kicked in World Cup '90 I went on television with a T-shirt message that read: KAISER FRANZ HAS NOT GOT A SINGLE HERR OUT OF PLACE. By the time this mauling of Yugoslavia was over a few million other people had joined me in thinking that West Germany were equipped to win the tournament.

The Germans looked awesome against a Yugoslavian side that many tipped as the best outsiders for the Cup. Long before the final whistle the Slavs looked like slaves who had been forced to work too hard by masters of the game of football.

I was looking for dynamic duo Rudi Voeller and Juergen Klinsmann to start the blitzkrieg, but it was West German skipper Lothar Matthaeus who electrified the game with two memorable goals. The Germans had been dictating the pace and the pattern of the match with a mixture of fluent and iron-hard football when Matthaeus struck his first goal in the 25th minute. Stefan Reuter telegraphed what he was about to do and chipped a pass through to his skipper, who turned and shot in one sweet movement to send the ball flashing left footed into the net from just outside the box.

Klaus Augenthaler was bossing the match from the back of the West German formation in a style reminiscent of "Kaiser" Franz Beckenbauer, who was looking on from the sidelines with a worried frown on his face. He was expecting big things from his team, and what looked excellent to English eyes was only just satisfactory to the *übermeister* of German football.

The Germans were pumping so many passes through the creaking Yugoslavian defence that it was only a matter of time before a second goal was added, Klinsmann duly obliging in the 40th minute with a glancing header across stranded goalkeeper Tomislav Ivkovic.

To their credit, outclassed Yugoslavia hung in like battered boxers seeking a clinch and they briefly saw the opening for a sneak punch in the 55th minute. Their gifted schemer Dragan Stojkovic, the victim of some hefty tackles that curbed his appetite for the action, floated in a free kick that Davor Jozic headed high into the net.

It was the only moment of joy that they were allowed. Matthaeus stepped back on to the scoring stage eight minutes later, racing on a zig-zagging run from the half-way line with the ball at his feet before rifling a right foot shot into the net from 20 yards. Then Rudi Voeller wrapped it up at 4–1, steering the ball into the net from close range after shell-shocked goalkeeper Ivkovic had made a mess of trying to hold a cross from Andreas Brehme.

Even perfectionist Franz Beckenbauer permitted himself a smile of satisfaction as the final whistle blew, and at home in England the bookmakers were sufficiently impressed by West Germany's performance to slash their odds from 7–1 to 4–1, and even then they looked a tasty bet.

Saint comments

With World Cup '90 just three days old it was already clear that Italy, West Germany and Brazil were the teams to watch. Holland were yet to unwrap their machine, but they were going to need to be at the top of their form to look more threatening than the three favourites.

I've had Greavsie chuntering on that West Germany will win the World Cup for weeks on end, and I have to agree the wee man is going to get a great run for his money.

As usual, the Germans are superbly organised and I was particularly impressed by the way Augenthaler kept dissecting the Yugoslav defence with long, piercing passes from a deep position. But to balance Greavsie's glowing report on Germany I have to say that the Yugoslavs were nothing like as inventive and industrious as we expected them to be. The Colombians, I felt, would give the Germans a better test.

Mo Johnston attempts an overhead kick against Costa Rica. As with most that Scotland tried in a match of agonising frustration, it came to nothing

 *Saint grieves*

Scotland gave one of the most pathetic and impotent performances in their history as they went down 1–0 to Costa Rica, a team that had qualified for the World Cup finals for the first time and were expected to play nothing more than a walk-on part in the greatest soccer show on earth.

We Scots seem to save our most embarrassing moments for the World Cup stage. In the past there have been humiliating experiences against the likes of Iran, Paraguay and Peru, but this defeat dragged us to an all-time low.

Scotland's form was so shaky going into the finals that we were mentally bracing ourselves for an unsuccessful tournament, but nothing could have got us prepared for this disgracefully inept display against opposition that was, frankly, nothing more than ordinary.

I have never seen a Scottish side so bereft of ideas and invention. You could count the number of times a player used skill to outwit an opponent on the fingers of a one-armed bandit. We employed novice-like hit-and-hope tactics, continually humping the ball into the goalmouth where goalkeeper Gabelo Conejo time and again proved reports that he was weak on crosses completely wrong.

During my playing days with Scotland I was lucky to have the service of wing wizards of the quality of Willie Henderson, Davie Wilson, Alex Scott and Johnny McLeod, and the jinking genius Jimmy Johnstone was running rings around full-backs for Celtic. It was obvious that Scotland should have been sending somebody down the flanks, but once Davie Cooper had pulled out with injury there was not a single wing specialist left in the squad.

I must be gracious to Costa Rica and place on record the fact that they played a neat and tidy game, but they were never put under the sort of pressure that could have torn their suspect defence apart. Scotland could claim that they were unlucky not to have turned one of their half -dozen chances into a goal, but in football you make your own luck and the Scots were so lacking in inspiration that they finally got what they deserved – nothing.

Costa Rica did half as much attacking, but achieved twice as much with sweeping floor passes that used to be a copyright of Scottish football. Their goal in the 48th minute was beautifully created and converted. Hector Marchena made a run at the heart of the Scottish defence before releasing a diagonal pass to Claudio Jara, who completely deceived his markers with the sweetest of backheels into the path of unattended Juan Cayasso. He coolly drilled the ball into the net with his left foot from seven yards as goalkeeper Jim Leighton dived in desperation at his feet.

I have rarely been so sickened by a result, and I could not see how Scotland were going to dig themselves out of the hole into which they had pushed themselves. They had lost not through lack of effort but through lack of quality. And that's a sad, sad statement to have to make about Scottish football.

 *Greavsie comments*

I have made something of a career of knocking Jock footballers, but I am really a closet fan and I was just as saddened as the Saint to see Scotland sink out of sight against Costa Rica.

Things might have been different if they had revealed the famous Scottish competitive spirit, but they were tame when compared with Costa Rican defender Mauricio Montero who tore into every tackle as if he was going to war. He was not a pretty sight, but he did a great job for his team and the pity was that the Scots had nobody who could match his drive and determination. I never thought I would say that of a Scottish team. How tragic.

Andy Roxburgh, Scotland's manager, who took the defeat with enormous dignity: "Dame Fortune was on the side of Costa Rica. We had so many chances but just could not finish. Their goalkeeper had a great game, but we could have won comfortably. To lose a match like this when you are hammering away non-stop is a major disappointment. But at the end of the day we have to put up our hands to what has happened and not look for excuses. I feel as if it's a bad dream, and today our emotions are bleeding. But it is not all over yet, and I must work at lifting the morale of the players. We're in the same boat as the likes of Argentina, Russia and Sweden. We've lost our first match. If we give our all in the next two games, who knows what will happen?"

Roy Aitken, Scottish skipper: "It was one of those games when just nothing would run for us. We had 80 per cent of the play, but the ball just refused to go into the net. The fans gave us tremendous support and we are all choked to have let them down. All we can do now is roll up our sleeves and try to make amends against Sweden."

Juan Cayasso, scorer of Costa Rica's goal: "That was the most important goal of my life. Brazil will obviously be harder to beat than Scotland, but our confidence is very high and we will not lie down without a fight. We are determined to make a good impression. This is our first experience of the World Cup and we're enjoying every second of it."

Bora Milutinovic, Costa Rica's Yugoslavian manager: "My instructions were that we should be patient. We knew Scotland would put us under a lot of pressure, but we remained calm and just looked for the opportunities to break out of defence. Scotland had more of the ball than we did, but we were more positive when it mattered."

 *Greavsie reports*

After the smoothness of Italy, the style of West Germany and the rhythm of Brazil it was embarrassing to watch the crudity of British football as England and Ireland kicked off their World Cup campaigns with a match that exposed all the warts and weaknesses of our game.

Remarkably, none of the previous eight ties in the tournament had ended in a draw despite pessimistic prophecies that this was going to be a defence-dominated World Cup.

But England and Ireland slugged out a draw in what was more a war of attrition than a game of football.

Canny Jack O'Charlton, full of blarney and baloney since he became manager of Ireland, kidded everybody that he was in the mood for a holiday rather than World Cup combat, but no manager gave a greater concentration on tactics. He knew he could not match England in the skill stakes and so brought them down to Ireland's level with a non-stop long-ball bombardment that meant spectators got a pain in the neck watching the action.

England could not have got off to a better start. Chris Waddle curled a cross against the strong wind in the eighth minute. Goalkeeper Pat Bonner decided to come off his line despite having two defenders guarding against trouble. All three of them could only look on as the alert Gary Lineker chested the ball down and then chased it into the net.

It was a tremendous psychological boost against an Irish team that had conceded only two goals during their previous 13 matches, and we settled back in anticipation of England rubbing out the memory of their defeat by Ireland in the European Championships two years earlier. But it was the Irish who grew in stature and confidence as they piled on pressure with a long-ball game that was ugly to the

eye but wearing on the limbs and lungs of the overstretched England defenders.

It was the 40th minute before England broke out of their heavily populated half to create another scoring chance, Lineker having a half-volley on the turn deflected over the bar by Kevin Moran.

There seemed to be a greater spirit running through the Irish team, and too many of the England players – in particular John Barnes and Peter Beardsley – were giving their impression of the Invisible Man. I had felt all along that Steve Bull should have started the match in place of Beardsley. It was the sort of helter-skelter, muscle-before-method football that would have suited his no-nonsense style.

Lineker was too often left to battle on his own. It would have been a different story if Bull had been operating alongside him and able to take advantage of some thoughtful probing passes by Paul Gascoigne, as he had against Czechoslovakia two months earlier.

Forked lightning lit up the stadium in spectacular fashion at the start of the wet and windy second half, but the football continued to be something out of the Dark Ages. England skipper Bryan Robson was giving his usual total effort, but he was restricted almost entirely to defensive duties because of the driving display in midfield by Paul McGrath, Ray Houghton, Andy Townsend and Kevin Sheedy.

For all their territorial advantage, Ireland did not create many clear chances and Peter Shilton, equalling Pat Jennings' world record of 119 international caps, was rarely called on to make a save.

On the hour, Chris Waddle at last unleashed one of his mazy runs and looked unlucky not to get a penalty when Moran stopped his rapid progress with a trip.

Jack Charlton, bidding to give a new dimension and impetus to Ireland's search for an equaliser, replaced John Aldridge with Alan McLoughlin in the 66th minute. Bobby Robson immediately countered by sending on Steve McMahon to keep an eye on McLoughlin. He substituted for Beardsley, who had been totally ineffective. McMahon, one of the most reliable players in the First Division, came cold into the cauldron and with his first touch of the ball lost control and watched in anguish

15

as his Merseyside neighbour, Everton's Kevin Sheedy, whipped it off his toes and planted an instant left-foot drive beyond the despairing dive of Shilton.

Nobody could dispute that Ireland deserved their equaliser, but it was cruel luck for McMahon who in a nightmare couple of minutes also managed to get himself booked.

Far too late, Bull was sent into the action with just six minutes to go. He came on as a substitute for the lion-hearted Lineker when it would have made more sense to have taken off the out-of-touch Barnes.

The draw was a moral victory for Ireland, but the match could be viewed as a defeat for British football (I know the Republic is not part of Britain, but their game was made in Britain, played by mainly British-reared footballers and plotted by a Geordie and a Devonian in coach Maurice Setters).

The standard of football was appalling, and the rest of the world looking on must have wondered if they were watching balloonists rather than footballers. While most of the teams in the finals had been playing the ball along the ground, England and Ireland concentrated on aerial attacks. We are light years behind the top countries, and when it comes to tactics we've got our heads in the clouds.

 *Saint comments*

England were so eaten up with the poverty of their own performance that not enough credit was given to Ireland for their whole-hearted display. They outran, outworked and often outwitted England, and it would have been a travesty if they had not come away with at least a point to show for their endeavour. I never expected a classic because there was too much at stake for both teams, but while every Irish player gave his all several of the English players should be asking themselves whether they had made a proper commitment to a game that will not live long in the memory.

Facing page: Gary Lineker forces the ball over the line for England's goal, with Mick McCarthy and Chris Morris in vain pursuit

Bobby Robson, England's manager, who had announced just days before the finals that he would be quitting his job after the World Cup to take charge of PSV Eindhoven: "I made the substitution to save the game and it cost us the game. I was responding to a tactical change made by Ireland. It was a pity that McMahon lost the ball to the wrong man. It fell to Sheedy's left foot and he is deadly with the cross shot and punished the mistake. We should have had a penalty when Chris Waddle was brought down but all in all I would not say it was a bad result. The main aim was not to get beaten. Now we have a point in the bag, and we know that if we can beat Holland or Egypt we will go through."

Steve McMahon, England's substitute: "My mistake cost us the game. I've apologised to the rest of the team. I just hope I get the chance to put it right. It was my first touch of the ball and I tried to play it to my right. The ball skidded off the pitch and flew away from my shins. It was just my luck that it fell to Kevin's left foot. He took the chance beautifully, and I was left feeling sick."

Jack Charlton, manager of Ireland: "Ours are not the best players in the world but they are certainly the most honest. We knew we would have to work hard against England. They have a great finisher in Lineker, two gifted runners in Waddle and Barnes and in Gascoigne probably a superstar of the future. We don't have players like that so we had no choice but to work hard. I think we allowed Barnes and Waddle just one cross each, and Lineker, being Lineker, took his one opportunity. We took the game to England for 90 minutes and deserved our point."

Peter Beardsley, England striker: "It was not very enjoyable out there on the pitch. It was like playing against Wimbledon."

Saint reports

 Greavsie reports

This match provided us with the real international flavour of World Cup football. South Korea's 1000 gong-bonging supporters brought a splash of colour to the Verona ground with their swirling Yin-Yang flags and huge red and white banners in Hangul script.

The Korean team went into a huddle on the pitch before the kick-off, but quickly looked as if they were going to come apart at the seams as the Belgians – in no mood to be the gentlemen of Verona – hit them with a bombardment that could and should have produced two goals within the first ten minutes.

But the Korean goal somehow survived this opening onslaught, and slowly but surely the Asians conquered their jangling nerves and hauled themselves into the game with neat counter-attacking football that was lacking only the final thrust in the penalty area.

Those of us who remembered the astonishing performances of North Korea on their way to the quarter-finals in the 1966 World Cup (when their bewildered victims included Italy) wondered if the South Koreans could conjure up a similar miracle. They were still in with a chance until the Belgians, brilliantly marshalled by Enzo Scifo, concocted an extraordinary goal in the 52nd minute. Goalkeeper Choi In-young came charging off his line to cut down the angle on Marc Degryse who was racing towards the Korean goal with the ball at his feet. Choi kept coming and coming and was outside the penalty area when Degryse released a chip that went higher than anything I have ever managed with a 9-iron before it landed in the unguarded Korean net.

The Koreans tried gallantly to battle back but ran out of heart and hope when Michel de Wolf netted a blistering shot from 25 yards in the 63rd minute. Belgium looked a sly fox of a side who could cause some surprises.

England manager Bobby Robson will have watched this match with knocking knees. Egypt, the team he would have been banking on to be a pushover, frightened the life out of Holland with a performance overflowing with flair and improvisation. The European champions were lucky to escape with a draw as Egypt flourished flowing, imaginative football surpassed so far in World Cup '90 only by Italy and Germany. It was difficult to believe that this was virtually the same team that England hammered 4–0 in Cairo four years ago.

The Dutch are notoriously unpredictable, and I sensed an undercurrent of dissatisfaction running through their team. They lacked real spirit and urgency and it added fuel to the stories that there has been unrest in the camp over team policy. Ruud Gullit, Marco van Basten and Ronald Koeman all revealed flashes of their unique talent, but it was never enough to put out the fire of the Egyptians and convince their supporters that they can, at last, mount a winning challenge for the World Cup.

It was totally against the run of play when substitute Wim Kieft slammed the ball into the roof of the net in the 58th minute after a mis-kick by Frank Rijkaard had momentarily brought disorder to a sound Egyptian defence.

There had been at least a dozen occasions when a mixture of luck, wild finishing and desperate defensive work had prevented Egypt from scoring. They finally got the goal they so richly deserved after Ronnie Koeman had tripped the always menacing Hossam Hassan. Abdel-Ghani put the penalty away into the corner of the net with as beautifully struck a spot-kick as I have ever seen.

Everybody thought Egypt had come to Italy just to make up the numbers. On this showing a lot of the favourites could find their numbers are up when they face them!

Saint reports

Uruguay scowled and scratched their way through the 1986 World Cup finals, making few friends but plenty of enemies with their cynical fouls. For World Cup '90 they have come up with a team that has swopped the snarl for a smile, and judging them on this opening display they will be exceptionally hard to conquer.

These were the last two of the 24 teams to show us their wares, and it was the first match to come up with a goalless stalemate. In past finals this would have been the norm for the opening games. Spain played unashamedly for the draw, but Uruguay were always looking for a scoring opportunity and in midfield juggler Enzo Francescoli – goal-poacher turned goal-maker – and striker Ruben Sosa they had two players who could emerge as major stars on the World Cup stage.

Spain countered with some elegant raids from the talented Emilio Butragueño, but he was too often left to hunt on his own by a Spanish side that revealed little apart from a desire not to be beaten. Their defensive work was efficient, and just occasionally verging on the evil. There were some nasty tackles going in, and Manuel Sanchiz paraded at the heart of the defence with a menacing 'thou shall not pass' attitude that made Uruguayan forwards think twice about trying to take on the Real Madrid master in man-to-man situations.

Sosa looked the man most likely to break the scoring deadlock, and you would have put your house (or your hacienda) on him to put the ball into the net when Uruguay were awarded a penalty after defender Perez Villaroya had handled on the goal-line in the 71st minute. For some reason Sosa elected to blast rather than place the ball and he looked on in horror as his shot ballooned over the bar. It would have won applause at Murrayfield. Uruguay

Manuel Sanchiz, who played for Spain with a menacing 'thou shall not pass' attitude

might be regretting this miss when the final group table decides who goes where in phase two. One goal can make all the difference to the chances of progress to the quarter-finals.

The conclusions I drew from this interesting rather than exciting match were that Uruguay are real dark horses for the Cup and that Spain are going to make life tough for everybody they meet. They showed only their defensive qualities. I reserve judgement until they decide to come out of their shell.

World Cup chat-a-thon

Well, Greavsie, we've seen all 24 teams now. This seems a good point to stop, catch our breath and have a chat about the tournament to date. What d'you think of it so far?

Rubbish, as my old mate Eric More-cambe used to say. Seriously though, I rate this a promising start to the World Cup finals. The football has generally been excellent, the crowd behaviour satisfactory, the refereeing firm but fussy, and the play sporting. Everything was fine until our lads came on to the pitch and trampled on all the good things that had gone before. Let's be honest, Saint, British football seems to be in a right old mess.

Aye, we've been a bit of a blot on the landscape so far. Let's just hope we improve in the next few games. If we don't the Scots *and* the English could be on the early plane home. From Scotland's point of view the defeat by Costa Rica has done untold damage to the morale of the team in Italy and, worse still, to the confidence of our game at home. We must start thinking about the entire structure of our game. For instance, should we abandon the idea of the Premier Division? I am sure that having so few teams in the main league is stunting our progress. With only ten clubs in the table the players are always involved in over-competitive derby matches in which everything is frantic and frenzied, and skill and quality take a back seat. They need room to breathe. We don't even have the excuse of losing our way because we are banned from Europe.

Being out of Europe has definitely been to the detriment of the game in England. We are still playing football that belongs to the Ice Age. We won't come in from the cold until we make vast improvement to our individual skills. It's our

"Don't switch him off yet. I want to read the next chapter."

technique that is being shown up in Italy as well as our naïve tactics. Too many of our players are needing two touches to control the ball, while even the Koreans and Egyptians, who are supposed to be backward at the game, have the basic skills to control the ball first time. There is nothing wrong with the long-ball game provided it is played positively and with flair, but against Jack O'Charlton's Ireland we seemed to be caught in two minds as to whether to try the skilful approach or the big boot. We finished up doing neither thing well. For the style we were trying to play it would surely have made sense to have selected Bull to start the match alongside Lineker.

I don't know about you, Greavsie, but I was embarrassed watching England and Scotland play. In England's match against Ireland the ball spent so much time in the air that I'm sure it must have made the hole in the ozone layer much bigger. And against Costa Rica, Scotland's passing was so predictable that they might just as well have sent a telegram to say what they were intending to do with the ball. All the scouting reports on the Costa Rican goalkeeper suggested he was like Dracula, frightened of crosses. But he held on to everything, and we kept feeding him the ball as if we were throwing fish to a seal. It was one of the most frustrating matches I have ever watched in my life. How did you feel watching England against Ireland?

I felt faint, Saint! No, airsick is the right description. The ball spent so much time in the air that a party of British holidaymakers got the best view – and they were flying home at the time. I think we should hold back on the GBH that we are dishing out to England and Scotland until the group matches are over, just in case they astound us with an amazing recovery. But the early signs are not good. How do you feel about your tip that Brazil are going to win the World Cup?

A little bit jittery. There were flashes of genius when they played Sweden, particularly from Careca but there were too many question marks about the defence for me to feel totally confident that they are going to make my forecast correct. I don't suppose you want to change your mind about West Germany winning the tournament?

You've got to be joking. Alongside Italy, they have been the most impressive team so far. The big bonus was the form of skipper Lothar Matthaeus. I knew he was an exceptional player, but I had considered him as more of a creator of chances for striking partners Juergen Klinsmann and Rudi Voeller rather than a goalscorer in his own right. His two goals against Yugoslavia were magnificent, one with the left foot and the other with his right. His all-round game was faultless, and Yugoslavia had no idea how to shut him out of the action. He is the jewel in Kaiser Franz's crown. It's early days yet, but he could easily emerge as the superstar of World Cup '90. Which individual has most taken your eye?

Giller

"Hey, Greavsie, d'you think I might have been watching too much World Cup football?"

There's Careca of Brazil and Matthaeus, of course. But the player who has most impressed me to date is Gianluca Vialli, who is the man who makes Italy tick. He's got great close control, is not frightened of taking on defenders with a mixture of pace and skill and he can lay on passes or go for goal himself. He was magnificent in Italy's opening performance that rivalled West Germany's as the best so far. Some of the passing of the Italians made them look like the dream machine, and what impressed me most of all was that they did not sit back and defend as so many Italian teams have done in the past. More teams in these group matches would have been more adventurous if FIFA had been sensible enough to award three points for a win and just one for a draw. I think we've got some negative games coming up.

That's enough of the chatting, Saint. You've got to catch the flight to Naples for Argentina's crucial match with the Soviets. We'll chat again after the group matches are over. Will England and Scotland have gone home by then? Will Cameroon still be over the moon? Watch this space.

21

Saint reports

Diego did it again! In the 1986 World Cup finals he scored a goal against England with his left hand. Here in Naples in World Cup '90 he *saved* a goal with his right!

Maradona was back helping out in defence in the 12th minute of a nerve-wracked match when he stuck out his arm to stop a goal-bound header from Soviet skipper Oleg Kuznetsov. It happened in the blinking of an eye and was missed by Swedish referee Erik Fredriksson, who did not have the benefit of action-replay facilities like us in the commentary boxes.

It was an eventful match for captain Maradona, who was playing in front of his adoring home fans in the Napoli stadium. He was one of five Argentinians booked, flitted in and out of the action like a butterfly and nursed his spluttering team to a victory that made some amends for the stunning defeat by Cameroon.

My impression was that Maradona was not 100 per cent fit, yet he still managed to play a critical part in Argentina's win that owed more to their determination than their undoubted skill.

Just two minutes before Maradona got away with his hand-ball Argentina suffered a crushing blow when their goalkeeper Nery Pumpido was carried off with a double fracture of his right leg after a sickening collision with teammate Juan Simon.

Sergio Goycochea proved a sound substitute goalkeeper and made a brilliant save late in the first half from Alexander Zavarov and another from Igor Dobrovolski in the second half, bravely smothering the loose ball after he had parried a first shot by Igor Shalimov.

Five changes from the team that kicked off the World Cup against Cameroon brought more cohesion to the Argentinian team, but there was still hesitancy and uncertainty in a defence that must improve considerably if it is not to be torn apart by more enterprising opposition than the Soviets, who were lacking individual flair and fire. Argentina were awarded a series of free kicks as the Soviets battled tenaciously to try to keep alive their fading hopes of surviving to the second phase. Jose Serrizuela went close with five ferocious long-range shots, but his free kicks – as with so many we have seen so far in the tournament – were predictable. It would have made more sense for Maradona to have tried his feared swerving shots, and the fact that he took few of the free kicks added to my suspicion that he was carrying a slight injury.

You could almost visibly see the world champions start to relax once they had taken the lead in the 30th minute. Julio Olarticoechea crossed from the left and Pedro Troglio, one of the five new faces brought into the team humbled by Cameroon, headed the ball firmly into the net past goalkeeper Alexander Uvarov, a surprise replacement for the highly rated Rinat Dasayev.

The Soviets had defender Vladimir Bessonov sent off three minutes into the second-half for blatantly pushing over the flying Claudio Caniggia. They battled to stay in the match but were finally counted out when Jorge Burruchaga netted three minutes from the end after Kuznetsov had been panicked into making an unwise back pass in his attempt to halt an attack that had been prompted by a super pass from Maradona.

 Greavsie comments

Argentina were looking like a giant that has been woken from a deep sleep. Their movements against the Soviets were creaky, but there was suffcient evidence to suggest they still have a lot to give before they will surrender their hold on the World Cup. They continue to lean too heavily on the marvellous talent of Maradona, who is not the force he was in 1986, but he still has match-winning power in that magical left foot of his.

The Soviets have not managed to get anywhere near the form that took them to the European Championship final two years ago.

Greavsie reports

The goalkeepers have brought a rainbow of colour to World Cup '90 with kaleidoscopic-style outfits that have turned the finals into a fashion show. In Rene Higuita Colombia have a goalkeeper whose personality matches the vivid, often silly colours that are being paraded. I have seen some crazy goalkeepers in my time, but Higuita beats them all. He played more as a sweeper than a 'keeper, often advancing as far as the half-way line to set up attacking movements. It injected entertainment into an undistinguished match, but if I had been one of his team-mates I would have wanted to shoot him for his eccentric behaviour. It's difficult enough to concentrate on playing World Cup football without having the distraction of your goalkeeper running around the pitch like a demented clown.

Colombia played a containing game, looking for the quick break, and they were worth a point for a spirited performance during which they were let down by their weak finishing. Carlos Valderrama came in for some rugged marking and failed to make his usual impact.

I was interested to see how Yugoslavia would react to their 4–1 drubbing by West Germany. They were my dark horses for the World Cup, and after an hour of neurotic football they at last started to stitch together the sort of movements that could yet give them a big say in these finals. Their talent is spread across Europe. They have two tremendously gifted players in French-based Dragan Stojkovic and Safet Susic, and it was Italian-based Davor Jozic who scored their crucial goal in the 73rd minute with a crashing volley. Seven minutes later the unconventional Higuita saved a weakly hit penalty by Faruk Hadzibegic , but Colombia did not have the fire- power to save the game.

Saint reports

You had to see it to believe it. Cameroon, shock conquerors of world champions Argentina in the first match of World Cup '90, collected the scalp of Romania to become – against all the odds – the first country to qualify for the second phase. The unflappable West Africans conjured an amazing climax to a match that had looked as if it was petering out to a tame goalless draw.

Roger Milla, at 38 the second-oldest player in the tournament to 40-year-old Peter Shilton, was summoned from the substitutes' bench in the 58th minute to try to give new drive and direction to the Cameroon attack. He had played in Cameroon's previous appearance in the World Cup finals in 1982 and was recalled to the squad in extraordinary circumstances.

He was winding down his career as a semi-professional with St Pierroise on the island of Réunion in the Indian Ocean when he was persuaded to return home by a call from Cameroon president, Paul Biya, who felt his country needed him after a disappointing showing in the African Nations Cup.

Milla made his presence felt in stunning style in the 76th minute when he steered the ball past goalkeeper Silviu Lung after getting the better of a duel with defender Ioan Andone. Ten minutes later, Milla raced smoothly into the penalty area, skipped to his right to make an angle for himself and then struck the sweetest of shots wide of Lung.

I could not help but feel sympathy for the Romanians, who must have found it difficult to get their minds off the new outbreak of political problems and violence in their homeland. They pulled back a goal in the 88th minute through Gavril Balint, but it was too little too late to stop the continuing fairy story of Cameroon.

Thursday June 14
Italy (1) **1, United States** (0) **0**
Group A, Rome

Giuseppe Giannini evades the lunging challenge of American defender Mike Windischmann before going on to score the match-winning goal for Italy

Greavsie reports

World Cup '90 should be subtitled "Tales of the Unexpected". What on paper looked to be a walk-over for Italy turned out quite differently on the pitch with the United States restoring their pride by holding them on a tight rein.

After the crushing defeat by Czechoslovakia in their first match I was convinced the United States would get taken apart by the Italians, who were superior in every department. The last time the two countries met in the World Cup finals was in Rome in 1934. Italy won 7–1 and the vast Roman crowd bayed for a repeat of that massacre.

Everything went to script when the multi-talented Giuseppe Giannini burst through the middle to score after ten minutes following a magnificent dummy by Gianluca Vialli. Then Vialli seemed sure to make it 2–0 when Nicola Berti earned a penalty, but the Sampdoria star continued his worrying goal famine by smacking the spot-kick against the left-hand post.

The Americans wisely massed in defence in their bid to avoid a repeat of the humiliation experienced against Czechoslovakia, and even the disappointed Italian fans had to applaud their bravery under a non-stop bombardment.

There was much to admire in Italy's approach play, and some of their passing movements were on a par with anything I have ever witnessed from the greatest teams of my lifetime. But it is a growing worry to them that they cannot find the back of the net as regularly as they will need to if they are going to capture the Cup. Once again Salvatore Schillaci came on as a lively subsitute for Andrea Carnevale and did enough to suggest he should have a permanent place in the shot-shy attack.

Saint reports

 Greavsie reports

Czechoslovakia gave a two-faced performance as they clinched a place in the second phase with this hard-earned victory over Austria. In the firs -half the Czechs unleashed the full range of their attacking skills that brought the reward of a half-time lead, but in the second half they went into their defensive shell as they protected their slender advantage.

It was a bruising battle, with Scots referee George Smith having to be quick on the draw with his cards to stop the match degenerating into a war.

Austria were my tip as the best long-shot for the Cup before the tournament started, but their promising forward line has failed to produce the expected fireworks. They had as much of the game as Czechoslovakia, particularly in the second half, but their finishing was frustratingly feeble.

Some of Czechoslovakia's attacking play in the first half suggested they have the ammunition to go all the way to at least the quarterfinals, and only Austria's irritating yet effective offside trap curbed them.

It was a mistake by Austria rather than Czech inspiration that led to the only goal of the match in the 30th minute. A suicidal back pass left goalkeeper Klaus Linberger with little alternative but to pull down Czech striker Jozef Chovanec, who damaged a thigh so badly in the incident that he was carried off on a stretcher. This has been the World Cup of missed penalties, but Michal Bilek made no mistake with his second successful spot-kick.

For Austria, the team with one of the strongest of all attacks, it has been a tournament of missed opportunities. It is a real puzzle how a side including class finishers like Gerhard Rodax and Toni Polster can still be goalless after two games. Surely they will break their duck against the United States. Surely.

Franz Beckenbauer's army marched into the second phase as they rolled over the outclassed United Arab Emirates with ruthless efficiency. The only surprise about the result is that the Germans did not at least double their score, this being due to some wild finishing in the first half-hour and some dogged defensive play by the Arabs.

The first half was played out to the accompaniment of claps of thunder and stair-rodding rain, and the Arabs must have thought they had been caught in a cyclone as West Germany applied heavy pressure right from the first kick.

There was a procession of incredible misses before Rudi Voeller at last got on the target in the 35th minute, nipping in between two defenders to clip in a centre from Juergen Klinsmann. Just 90 seconds later Klinsmann rose unchallenged to head in a cross from Stefan Reuter.

A feature of the West German play, and something to be watched and enjoyed in the later stages, was the combined attacking play of skipper Lothar Matthaeus and of left-back Andreas Brehme, who is as accomplished an overlapping defender as I have ever seen. His ball control would put most forwards to shame.

There was a rare lapse of concentration by Germany's defenders early in the second half that let Khalid Mubarek in for the first ever goal by the Emirates in a World Cup finals. They had just got over their celebrations when Matthaeus restored the two-goal advantage with a snap shot that was deflected into the net.

Uwe Bein made it 4–1 with a crackerjack of a shot from 25 yards, and Voeller rounded off the scoring with a powerful header that went into the net off the arm of an Arab defender. Once again the Germans had looked awesome.

25

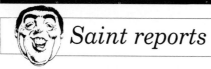

Saint reports

There has got to be an amazing transformation in the way Brazil are playing if they are to carry my forecast as the eventual winners any further than the quarter-finals. Tradition demands that we always look to Brazil to bring flair and style to the World Cup stage, but for World Cup '90 they have sent a team of artisans rather than artists.

They were never in any danger of losing this match against Costa Rica, but they muddled rather than moulded their way to victory. After two looks at them I would like to switch to tipping West Germany as the likely winners, but Greavsie would never let me get away with that. So I am lumbered with Brazil, and even after two victories they have done nothing to fill me or their huge army of yellow-clad supporters with confidence.

Even their one world-class player, Careca, lost his way against a Costa team that came only to survive, and he was substituted ten minutes from the end by hot prospect Bebeto. It would be an understatement to say that I am disappointed with Brazil, and what was particularly sad was to see their players arguing among themselves as movements broke down. That is a bad sign, and suggests the team spirit is not all that it should be.

Costa changed into the black and white striped shirts so familiar at Turin on the backs of local favourites Juventus. The black stripes must have looked like prison bars to the Brazilians during the frustrating first half-hour when they struggled to break through Costa's disciplined nine-man defence.

I was just beginning to despair of Brazil finding the key to unlock the Costa safe when Muller stooped low in the 33rd minute to shoot towards the net from 12 yards after a Jorginho long throw from the right had caused confusion. The ball got two deflections on the way into the Costa net. It was a messy goal that reflected the overall Brazilian performance.

Five minutes later goalkeeper Gabelo Conejo made a spectacular flying one-handed save to turn off target a whiplash 20-yard free kick from Branco. This was the best of a handful of goal efforts by Brazil during a first half in which they looked little better than ordinary. Admittedly Costa were making it hard for them to play by closing down all free space, but the Brazil sides we have been used to seeing in the past would have skilfully picked a path through to goal.

Valdo came from deep positions to unleash two fine goal attempts in the second half, and Conejo did well to block a close-range shot from Alemao after the Brazilian had danced past three tackles in a rare moment of magic. Careca saw a header hit the under-side of the bar as Brazil maintained the pressure, restricting Costa to just one scoring chance. It was a workmanlike performance, but we expect sorcery not sweat from the boys from Brazil.

Now I wait anxiously to see how Scotland perform against them.

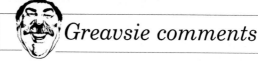

Greavsie comments

Pelé is in Italy working as a television summariser (the things we old pros do to earn a crust). It must make him shudder to see what Brazil '90 are producing under the guise of football. They are the least effective Brazilian team to compete in a World Cup finals, yet I have a funny feeling they could battle their way through to the late stages. What they lack in skill they make up for with steel. Take it from me, this is a team that could look after itself in a rough-house. They are just not pretty to watch.

All we can hope is that they get into their smooth, samba stride in the second phase because this World Cup needs a sparkling Brazil team. The tournament started with a bang and seemed to run a little out of steam in the last few matches we have seen. There would be nothing better to give it a new lease of life than a Brazil team producing exciting Latin-beat football in the old-fashioned way.

Saturday June 16
Scotland (1) **2**, **Sweden** (0) **1**
Group C, Genoa

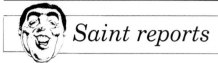 *Saint reports*

Scotland walked tall from a game they had to win to repair their self-respect and to rekindle their hopes of making progress into the second phase of World Cup '90. They did themselves and every one of the 15,000 Scottish supporters in the Genoa stadium proud with a performance that lessened the agony of their defeat by Costa Rica.

Stuart McCall and Mo Johnston, two red-headed players who covered the pitch like the fire from a flame-thrower, emerged as the goal-scoring heroes, but this was very much a team triumph for which manager Andy Roxburgh deserves hearty praise.

Roxburgh worked wonders to pick up his players after their spirit had been shattered by the humiliating loss to Costa Rica. His team rebuilding was bold and positive. He relegated Paul McStay and Jim Bett to the sidelines and selected a battling midfield four of Roy Aitken, McCall, Murdo MacLeod and Gordon Durie. They laid the foundations for victory by strangling Swedish progress with good old-fashioned harassing and chasing, while behind them the back line of defenders drove long balls up to the front runners Johnston and Robert Fleck. This was made-in-Scotland football that was played with the drive and tenacity that had been so sadly missing against the Costa Ricans.

It was a dream World Cup debut for Fleck. Summoned from his holiday in Yugoslavia as a late addition to the squad and picked in preference to Ally McCoist, he helped set up Scotland's first goal in the tenth minute by forcing a corner after the industrious Durie had worried Sweden with a powerful run down the left.

MacLeod's corner-kick was flicked on by Dave McPherson, and McCall lunged forward to stab the ball over the Swedish goal-line with three defenders surrounding him. You could see the Scots visibly grow in confidence with this precious lead under their belts, and they prevented Sweden from getting into their smooth stride by challenging fiercely for every ball.

The Swedes had impressive Liverpool defender Glenn Hysen back at the heart of their defence after injury, and he was given a torrid time as Johnston and Fleck snapped at his heels like Scottish terriers. I was particularly impressed by the output of Gordon Durie, who covered marathon distances at sprinter's speed and always had the Swedish defence at full stretch when he took them on with probing runs from his midfield base.

Tomas Brolin, Sweden's outstanding prospect, was given little chance by the quick-tackling Scottish defenders to show his precocious talent. He looked set to score an equaliser early in the second half, but the poised and commanding Craig Levein got Scotland out of trouble with a superbly timed challenge.

It was always a rugged man's match, and McPherson was booked in the 68th minute following a clash with Joakim Nilsson as the Swedes picked up the pace in an effort to save the game.

The Swedes sent on Glenn Stroemberg as a substitute for Peter Larsson to give a lift to their feverish hunt for an equaliser. Andy Roxburgh responded by pitching Paul McStay into the action as a replacement for Durie, who had gone beyond the call of duty with his all-out performance.

Sweden were leaving inviting gaps in their defence as they pushed forward, and McCall was quick to see an opening through which he steered a perfect pass for Johnston, whose shot hit the legs of goalkeeper Thomas Ravelli.

Just as it began to look as if Scotland had used up all their energy keeping the Swedes at bay they were given breathing space when Roland Nilsson up-ended skipper Aitken in the penalty area as he attempted to put the finishing touch to a sweeping move involving Alex McLeish and Fleck. Johnston took the 78th-minute penalty and made nothing of the enormous pressure on his shoulders as he

banged home the most crucial spot-kick of his career.

All credit to Sweden. They refused to admit defeat and came battling back to snatch a goal in the 85th minute when Stroemberg, a striking figure with shoulder-length hair and a Viking beard, got on the end of a cross-field pass from Stefan Schwarz to send the ball wide of Jim Leighton, who had been in sound form.

Scottish hearts stopped in the last minute when the Swedes again bundled the ball into the net but this time from an offside position. At the final whistle Andy Roxburgh paid tribute to Scotland's "twelfth man" – the Scottish supporters who had buried all their anger over the defeat by Costa Rica and got right behind their team. Andy triumphantly waved a tartan scarf in their direction and was greeted with a Hampden Park-size roar in return.

It was quite a night for Scotland, the team that had come back from the dead.

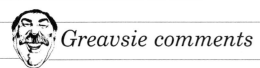 ## Greavsie comments

Only dear old Scotland would muck us about like this. They were atrocious against Costa Rica, but then against Sweden produced the sort of passion and commitment we have traditionally associated with great Scottish sides.

I admired the way Andy Roxburgh conducted himself following the defeat by Costa Rica that would have had many managers reaching for the suicide pills. But he kept his nerve, passed his quiet confidence on to his players and boldly picked a team to do the job he had in mind.

This victory was achieved against a Swedish defence that shut out England in two goalless draws on the road to the finals of World Cup '90. Now it is going to be fascinating to see if the Scots can achieve what seemed the impossible by collecting one, or even two points against Brazil. Having watched the Brazilians give a stuttering display against Costa Rica, I feel Scotland could yet qualify for the second phase for the first time in their history.

Facing page: Tigerish Mo Johnston forces Glenn Hysen into making a desperate tackle

QUOTE UNQUOTE

Andy Roxburgh, Scotland's manager: "I bet the Brazilians cringed when they were watching us tonight. They now know they are going to be in for a real battle when we meet in Turin on Wednesday. Every one of our players was a hero. They gave us everything, and in terms of commitment and effort they were simply magnificent. I hope our fans are as proud of us as we are of them. They got behind us like no other supporters could. It was incredible. There was no way we could let them down. Now we need them behind us again in Turin when we face Brazil. We have never beaten them, but there is a first time for everything. The Brazilians have weaknesses. It is going to be up to us to try to expose them. We know we face a mountain but this victory over Sweden has given us the determination to try to climb it. We hope we have made a lot of people eat their words following their criticism of our performance against Costa Rica, which – let's be honest – was a game we deserved to win by at least two or three goals."

Alex McLeish, Scottish player of the year: "Andy Roxburgh really got us wound up for this one. He told us to treat it like a British Cup Final, and we all gave it every ounce of effort. Sweden can take you apart if you give them the chance, but we refused to let them play and kept them under pressure with what was full-blooded Scottish football."

Mo Johnston, scorer of Scotland's vital penalty: "I didn't stop to think of the pressure on me. All my concentration was on making sure I got the ball into the net. There have been quite a few penalties missed in these finals. I was determined not to add to the list."

Olle Nordin, Sweden's manager: "Scotland fought like tigers and deserved their victory. They will give Brazil a fright. The support they got from their fans was remarkable."

29

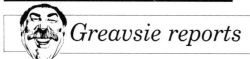

Greavsie reports

Bobby Robson took my breath away with the boldest team selection of his managerial career, and then England proceeded to leave Holland breathless with an exhibition of excellence that lacked only the deserved reward of a goal.

This was just about the most encouraging display I have seen from an England team under the Robson banner, and there was enough flair and finesse to suggest they could be serious challengers for the trophy if they can get through this tightest of all the groups.

The remarkable thing was that they produced their world-class performance using the sweeper system that Robson has virtually ignored throughout his reign as England manager.

Excuse me blowing my trumpet, but I have been advocating the sweeper system for England for two years – since England's abysmal showing in the 1988 European Championship finals. I have argued the case that Bryan Robson should be dropped back behind the last line of defence in the sort of role Franz Beckenbauer perfected with West Germany and Bayern Munich.

Not having even experimented with the formation during the build-up to World Cup '90, I did not believe Robson would be adventurous enough to gamble on introducing the system in the finals. How wrong can you be?

The player he chose for the job was Derby central defender Mark Wright, who was recalled for his first international since England's defeat by Holland in the European Championships. Paul Parker came in for Gary Stevens at right-back and Peter Beardsley was, as anticipated, the odd man out from the

Facing page: Peter Shilton calls for calm in his record 120th international appearance

Paul Gascoigne, who "came of age" with a world-class performance against Holland

team so heavily criticised after the draw with Ireland in the opening match.

The game was barely ten minutes old when first John Barnes and Gary Lineker and then Paul Gascoigne and Bryan Robson combined to threaten the Dutch goal.

This was the match in which 'Gazza' Gascoigne came of age as an international player. He strode around the centre stage as if he owned it, and some of his forward surges and his passes were world class in their quality and execution. One twisting turn on the ball when he foxed two Dutch defenders in the second half was out of the Johan Cruyff school of skill and earned appreciative applause even from the Dutch supporters who recognise genius when they see it.

It was not a one-sided match as is the impression I am probably giving, but England were always that little bit sharper and hungrier for the ball. Holland are still not firing on all cylinders, and Ruud Gullit looks as if he is

31

several games short of real match fitness. Just as disappointing for the Dutch has been the unimpressive form of Marco van Basten, who was shut out of the action by the expert marking of the immaculate Des Walker.

There is no doubt that the springboard for England's excellent showing against Holland was a defence in which Mark Wright was outstanding in his unfamiliar role as the sweeper. His presence at the back seemed to give all his team-mates that extra confidence to try to put skill first, because they knew if they made a mistake there was going to be the safety net of the sweeper system to help get them out of trouble.

Peter Shilton, overtaking the world record of Pat Jennings with his 120th international appearance, was rarely troubled by the Dutch attack and seemed extremely comfortable with his Derby team-mate Wright in calling distance.

Bobby Robson again displayed uncustomary boldness when he sent Steve Bull on as a substitute for the ineffective Chris Waddle with nearly half an hour to go. It was an ambitious change that almost brought the reward of an instant goal when Lineker found Bull with a superb through pass, but the aggressive Wolves striker headed over the bar.

Lineker himself had missed a golden opportunity when he sliced his shot wide after an exchange of passes with Barnes tore the Dutch defence wide open. He also raised false hopes in the 53rd minute when he steered the ball into the net, only to have the goal disallowed because he had controlled it with his left arm. Maradona he ain't!

Of the four Dutch "masters" only Frank Rijkaard was at the peak of his form, but he was so busy helping to control England at the back that he was rarely able to make a telling contribution to the attack. Ronald Koeman was also restricted to desperate defensive work against an England attack often boosted by the overlapping runs of right-back Paul Parker, who gave the team a new dimension with his inventive play.

There was a blow for England when injury-prone skipper Bryan Robson had to go off in the 65th minute with an Achilles problem after forcing himself to play following a pain-killing injection on a damaged toe. Again Bobby Robson showed a surprising spirit of adventure, replacing his captain with the attacking David Platt rather than with the more obvious choice of Steve McMahon. Platt settled in immediately with confidence and composure.

With 15 minutes to go Holland sent Wim Kieft on as substitute for Johnny van't Schip alongside van Basten, but it was England who were applying pressure at the end.

There was a dramatic climax. Stuart Pearce drove a last-minute free kick from out on the right wide of the Dutch defensive wall and straight into the net past diving goalkeeper Hans van Breukelen. Celebration of a winning goal was cut short when the referee made it clear that he had awarded an indirect free kick. The ball could only have missed the fingers of van Breukelen by inches. England came that close to what would have been a richly deserved win. They've put the spring back into the step of English football.

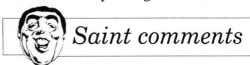 *Saint comments*

I am not sure whether it was boldness or desperation that made Bobby Robson go for a sweeper system that he has studiously ignored in the past. Whatever it was, it worked and it has given England a new shape and dimension. They must surely continue with the formation after its success against Holland, and if they can get through to the second phase it could make them extremely difficult to beat.

It may bring about a revolution in British football because League clubs have been unenthusiastic about introducing a sweeper system that is widely used throughout Europe. If it works for England, then expect it to be copied in the League next season, just as Ramsey's "wingless wonders" formation brought an army of imitators after the World Cup win of 1966.

We will be much wiser after England's final group match against Egypt, but all the signs are that they have found the style and the confidence to make it through to the second phase. Holland were again disappointing, but they just might be waiting to pick up their pace in time for the vital stages of the finals.

Marco van Basten has Stuart Pearce (left) and Des Walker to contend with as he tries to find a way through the England defence

QUOTE UNQUOTE

Bobby Robson, England's manager: "I knew that I would have taken enormous stick if the changes had not worked and we had lost. But that's what managing is all about. You have to take bold decisions regardless of what other people might think. The only pity is that an excellent England performance was not rewarded with a victory. I must single out the performance of Paul Gascoigne. He was absolutely outstanding, and it was a pleasure to watch him on the ball. Mark Wright did a fine job as our sweeper, as I knew he would. I hope that people will now share my faith in English football. We have players with fine technique. The match against Ireland was a one-off. Jack Charlton's team will make it difficult for any side to play. I'm going to be fascinated to see how Holland cope with them. The bad news tonight is that our captain Bryan Robson has an Achilles tendon injury. We will rest him for the next few days in the hope we can get him fit for the match against Egypt."

Peter Shilton, England's record-breaking goalkeeper: "We have now found a system that all clubs in the First Division should play next season. Having a sweeper encourages skill and makes the team more efficient."

Gary Lineker, England striker: "On another night I could have had a couple of goals. My luck deserted me."

Hans van Breukelen, Holland goalkeeper: "Stuart Pearce admitted to me that he blasted his free kick in the hope that somebody would touch it on its way into the net. But we knew it was an indirect free kick. England played very well. We were impressed. It is going to be a tough game for us against Ireland."

33

Saint reports

 Greavsie reports

Egypt lost many of the friends they had made with their skilful showing against Holland by sucking the life from this game with a dull and dreary defensive display. They settled for a draw long before the final whistle and aggravated everybody in general and Jack Charlton in particular with unashamed time-wasting tactics.

Big Jack got himself drawn into an after-match dispute following his disparaging remarks about Egypt's attitude. "I hate teams like that," he fumed. "I deplore them. I've seen results that were amazing over the years, but I've never played a team that did not try to create a single chance in 90 minutes. I didn't like the game, I didn't like the way Egypt played, I didn't like their time-wasting. I didn't like anything. If you come to a World Cup you should at least try to play a bit of football. Egypt didn't attempt to do anything but defend."

It was tough stuff from Jack, and the Egyptians didn't take kindly to what he had to say. He was accused of "arrogance and racism" and of "losing his balance".

I could understand how Jack, to whom I was coach at Sheffield Wednesday, felt. He likes an honest approach to the game, and Egypt could have been accused of cheating with their time-wasting as they strangled any chances Ireland had of winning the game.

Mainly because of the way Egypt decided to play it, the match was just one long traffic jam in the heavily populated corridor between the penalty areas. It was the worst match of the finals to date.

Ireland now have to play out of their skins against Holland in a repeat of the final group match in the European Championships two years ago when the Dutch were lucky to win by a late goal.

The Saint described Belgium as a sly fox of a side after their 2–0 victory over South Korea, and that's exactly what they looked against Uruguay in a magnificent match in Verona during which the accent was on attractive, attacking football. Despite their 3–1 defeat, Uruguay seemed the superior side and could yet prove a surprise package in the later rounds.

The Uruguayans were beaten by a team that took its chances brilliantly and then craftily worked at maintaining their advantage in the face of a fierce fight back by the South Americans during which they produced some of the finest football of the finals.

Leo Clijsters gave Belgium a 14th-minute lead with a classically constructed goal, putting the finishing touch with a deft header to a sweeping movement that left the Uruguayan defenders tackling shadows. Six minutes later Belgium's majestic play-maker, Italian-born Enzo Scifo, netted with a low sniper shot from all of 30 yards. Uruguay were rocked back on their heels, but then unleashed a sustained series of attacks that had the Belgian defence stretched to breaking point. All that was missing was the vital finishing touch.

Belgium, concentrating on quick, crafty breaks, appeared to have made the game safe two minutes into the second half when veteran Jan Ceulemans drove the ball into the net from the edge of the penalty area.

Eric Gerets, rugged Belgian defender, was ordered off after collecting a second booking, and Uruguay increased the pressure as they boldly tried to get back into a game that lesser teams would have given up as lost. They were at last rewarded for their stunning football when substitute Pablo Bengoechea netted in the 72nd minute. We may not have heard the last of these multi-talented but moody Uruguayans.

Sunday June 17
South Korea (1) **1, Spain** (1) **3**
Group E, Udine

Spanish forward Francisco Villaroya performs his version of the familiar and frustrating World Cup '90 dive after a challenge from Hwang Bo-kwan

 Saint reports

Real Madrid striker Michel revealed why he is one of the highest-paid footballers in Spain by conjuring the first hat-trick of World Cup '90. South Korea were the unlucky team on the receiving end, and they will be packing their bags for an early exit from a tournament in which they were simply outgunned.

Michel opened his account in the 22nd minute when he volleyed in a cross from Perez Villaroya. The Koreans kept their heads, and their neat passing game brought the reward of an equaliser two minutes before half-time. Hwang Bo-kwan found the top left-hand corner of the Spanish net from 25 yards.

The Koreans stepped up the tempo of their game in the second half, and Kim Joo-Sung gave the Spanish defence a fright in the 50th minute with a dazzling run in which he whipped the ball past five opponents. But the Koreans lacked the sort of devastating finishing punch that Michel provided for Spain. In the 62nd minute he made the Koreans regret their lack of height in defence when he bent a freekick over the top of their wall and into the net. It was a stunning piece of accuracy and suggested that Spain could have the ammunition at last to make a major impact on the world stage.

Their domestic football is as good as any in the world, but they never seem to reach their potential in World Cup competition. Michel completed his hat-trick with a gem of a goal in the 80th minute, ghosting past three Korean defenders before netting with a perfect left-foot shot. It was not a vintage performance by Spain, but a great improvement on their showing against Uruguay.

35

Monday June 18	Monday June 18
USSR (2) **4, Cameroon** (0) **0**	**Argentina** (0) **1, Romania** (0) **1**
Group B, Bari	Group B, Naples

 ## *Saint reports*

 ## *Greavsie reports*

The Soviets found their shooting boots too late to save them from an early elimination, but at least they walked out with their heads held high after doing considerable damage to the confidence of Cameroon. They exposed the weaknesses of the Africans, who it seems may have produced their peak performances in their first two games when they were an unknown quantity.

It was difficult to believe that this was the same Cameroon side that shocked the stuffing out of Argentina and got the better of Romania. Perhaps they switched off mentally because they knew they had already qualified, but whatever the reason they looked more like the sort of side we expected before the start of World Cup '90.

Their defence was as wide open as a barn door against a Soviet side showing far more pace and imagination than in either of their previous two matches. It must have been really frustrating for the Soviets to have found their rhythm too late to make a telling impact in a tournament for which they were one of the favourites following their powerful performances in the European Championships.

They took a deserved lead in the 20th minute when Oleg Protasov netted from close range following a low cross from the right. It was the first time Cameroon had trailed in the championship and you could almost see the morale seeping out of their players.

Andrei Zygmantovich made it 2–0 nine minutes later, driving the loose ball into the net after Sergei Aleinikov had hammered a rising shot against the bar. Alexander Zavarov and Igor Dobrovolski added second-half goals, but when they heard the result of the drawn Argentina–Romania match the Soviets sadly realised they had left their goal barrage too late and were off home with the also-rans.

Diego Maradona, one of the greatest footballers ever to pull on a pair of boots, worries me as World Cup '90 reaches the half-way stage. He has so far been unrecognisable as the ball-conjuring master who monopolised the 1986 finals, and his main energy seems to have been confined to trying to convince referees that he is more sinned against than sinning.

Maradona tumbled to the floor no fewer than 22 times during a match that blew hot and cold and in which both teams seemed to settle for a draw that guaranteed them a place in the second phase.

On just half a dozen occasions Maradona was the victim of tough tackles; most of the other times he was giving a theatrical mime of a dying swan as he attempted to persuade the referee that he had been the victim of violence. If Argentina are to make any more progress in this tournament they need Diego to start playing as only he can and to leave the play-acting to others less gifted in the true arts of the game. I feel strongly that the professional fall should be treated as harshly as the professional foul, and Maradona should be given his marching orders if he continues to try to con referees.

I was delighted for Romania that they have survived to the second phase. With their country on the brink of a civil war it must be enormously difficult to concentrate on playing football. In Marius Lacatus and Gheorghe Hagi they have two players who are better at playing the game than most and with artists of this quality in their team they could yet go at least as far as the quarter-finals.

Both goals came in the second half, Pedro Monzon heading in a swerving Maradona corner in the 62nd minute and Gavril Balint equalising six minutes later after a charging run by Lacatus.

Saint reports

Colombia saved their World Cup life with a dramatic injury-time equaliser as they exposed the West Germans as being mere mortals and not the supermen they had looked in their first two matches. A match brimming over with exciting, inventive football was marred by the play-acting of the Colombians, who feigned injuries as if they had been shot.

For most of the game the South Americans looked the more fluent and creative team, but they stretched the patience of the spectators and the referee close to breaking point with their tiresome antics. Skipper Carlos Valderrama cannot be missed on a football pitch because of his bouquet of orange hair that makes him look like a children's doll, but he was even more noticeable in this game because of a farcical incident just before half-time.

He went down as though pole-axed after an innocuous tackle by Klaus Augenthaler. Northern Ireland referee Alan Snoddy was close to the action at the moment of impact and waved play on, satisfied that Valderrama was not injured. Valderrama lay there for fully three minutes until Snoddy was forced to stop play and call on the trainer. Then four stretcher bearers were summoned and the Colombian captain was carried off with spectators wondering how on earth he had sustained such a serious injury. Three minutes later Valderrama came bouncing back into the match like a spring lamb, and our first suspicions that he had not been badly hurt were confirmed. From then on, every time the enormously talented Valderrama touched the ball he was greeted with shrieks of derisive whistling and jeering from all but the Colombian supporters. It is this sort of feigning that has dropped a large black cloud on what has been to date an otherwise satisfactory tournament.

The ridiculous thing is that all the Colombians achieved with their play-acting was to upset their own rhythm. If they had just concentrated on playing the game they might easily have given the West Germans their first defeat of the tournament.

Carlos Estrada and Luis Fajardo looked as clever and skilful as any forwards in the finals as they teased and tormented the Germans with dazzling ball control. The German defenders were often run dizzy by a combination of dribbles and first-time passing that made you wonder whether it was the South Americans who were really the favourites to win the World Cup.

For the first time we were forced to wonder whether the German defence is good enough to hold out under prolonged pressure. Augenthaler looked a little on the slow, lumbering side in his sweeping role, and skipper Lothar Matthaeus revealed a brittle temperament as things started to go wrong behind him. He kept up a non-stop tirade of complaints to the referee, which was a tell-tale sign that the Colombians had him and his team-mates rattled.

Colombia might have had three goals during a purple patch in the first half. Fajardo had a close-range shot saved by goalkeeper Bodo Illgner and then missed a sitter after Estrada and Valderrama had combined to carve open the German defence. Freddy Rincon, withdrawn to a base in midfield to make room for the inclusion of Estrada and Fajardo, outwitted two defenders to set up a chance for Estrada, who headed inches over the bar.

Franz Beckenbauer was hopping around on the touchline like a cat on a hot tin roof, and he sent veteran Pierre Littbarski on as a substitute at the start of the second half to try to change the pattern and pace of the match. Still the Colombians continued to dominate, and it was all the Germans could do to stay in the match.

But then, as we have seen so many times in the past with German sides, their tremendous character and discipline began to pay dividends. Slowly but surely they started to drag themselves into the game. The Colombians had made the mistake of taking their foot off the accelerator and settling for a draw. The Germans saw their opportunity and started to pour forward. With 15 minutes left to play

Matthaeus lobbed the ball against the cross-bar. Then Rudi Voeller shaved the post with a cross shot.

In the 88th minute Littbarksi snatched what we all thought was the winning goal when he netted with a fierce left-foot shot. There seemed no way back for Colombia, who had hit the Germans with every conceivable attacking ploy without the reward of a goal.

The game was into its second minute of injury time when Valderrama found one more way through the German defence. His delicate pass into the path of Rincon carried perfect pace and weight. Goalkeeper Illgner came racing off his line to try to cut out the danger, but Rincon kept his head and calmly slotted a low shot through Illgner's legs and into the back of the net.

The Colombians celebrated as if they had just won the World Cup. They thoroughly deserved their draw, but they would have been even more warmly welcomed into the second phase if they had cut out the irritating play-acting.

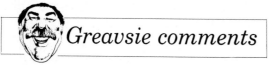 *Greavsie comments*

Colombian manager Francisco Maturana produced two hidden aces with the sudden appearance of Carlos Estrada and Luis Fajardo, who had been sitting out the World Cup on the touchline bench. Both players looked stunningly gifted, and their performances against the Germans made everybody wonder why they had not been called on to play before.

There were a lot of questions asked of the German defence for the first time in the tournament, and – like the Saint – I was worried about the seeming lack of mobility of Augenthaler at the back. He is a fine prompter of attacks, but dodgy when it comes to defensive duties. Even though the Germans were often in danger of being pulled apart by the Colombians, they still had the class and the character to battle back to grab control of the game. I remain happy to tip them for the Cup, but let's keep an eye out for Colombia. They are immensely talented but can be tripped up by their temperament.

Franz Beckenbauer, West Germany's manager: "It was not a particularly satisfying performance by my team. We were not as sharp and as alert as we have been. A psychological factor came into it. We were relaxed mentally because we had already qualified for the second phase. I sent Pierre Littbarski on to give us a new dimension in the second half. The Colombians played some magnificent football, and they will give any team they meet a very hard time. They play with flair and their passing is fast and accurate. I do not wish to get drawn into the controversy about Valderrama. All I wish to say is that the refereeing in the tournament has been inconsistent. As Valderrama did not get up I assumed he was injured. We are very happy to be playing our next match in Milan bcause we feel so at home here. We have made a very good start, but our real test starts now. There are some excellent teams going through to the next phase."

Francisco Maturana, Colombia's manager: "We are filled with joy to have forced a draw with a team as great as West Germany. It would have been an injustice had we lost. I cannot understand why there is all this fuss about Valderrama. It is a doctor you should ask about whether he was hurt. I don't see that it is particularly important. What is important is that we have done enough to qualify for the second phase. It is going to be very difficult from now, but we are happy because we have already acquitted ourselves well. We have had many messages of congratulations from home in Colombia. We have made them happy. That is what is important."

Carlos Valderrama, Colombia's captain: "Of course I was injured and needed treatment. It was not my idea to bring on a stretcher. The referee should have stopped the game immediately. Physiotherapists not referees should decide whether a player is injured."

Dragan Stojkovic, one of the tournament's most gifted players, plots a path through the Emirates defence as he shows the skill that is valued at £7million on the transfer market

Greavsie reports

Yugoslavia qualified for the second round of the finals with a thumping victory over a United Arab Emirates team that came, saw and was conquered. They go home to the Emirates a little bruised and a lot wiser about world football, and I am sure we will see them back as a much more powerful footballing nation at a World Cup tournament in the not too distant future.

Two goals by Darko Pancev, a precocious young talent from Red Star Belgrade, and a goal apiece by Safet Susic and the powerful Robert Prosinecki lifted Yugoslavia to the win they needed to guarantee a place in the second phase for the first time since 1974.

But the architect of their victory does not appear on the scoresheet. Dragan Stojkovic had a hand, or rather a well-directed foot, in all four goals, and dominated and directed the game like a traffic cop from his midfield base. It was easy to see why Marseille have parted with £7million to pair Stojkovic with Chris Waddle on the French football stage.

The Emirates, 2–0 down inside the first ten minutes, responded with a golden goal by striker Ali Thani Jumaa in the 21st minute. I call it a golden goal because his reward from a well-wisher at home was a Rolls Royce. His team-mate, Khalil Ghanim, would not have earned himself even an old banger when he foolishly got himself sent off for kicking Pancev in the closing stages. It was a sad way for the Emirates to finish their World Cup campaign.

It will be fascinating to see how Yugoslavia fare in the next round. They have individuals with the skill to match the best players, but their teamwork is too often disjointed.

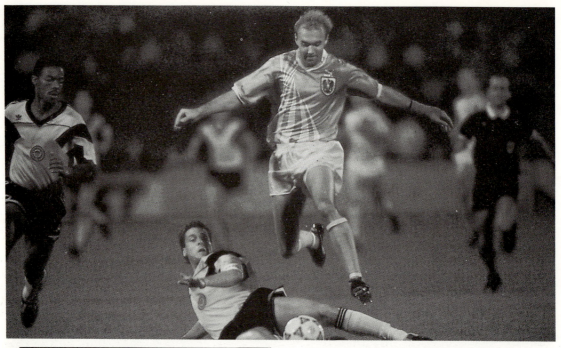

Tuesday June 19
Austria (0) **2**, **United States** (0) **1**
Group A, Florence

Gerhard Rodax hurdles over a tackle from American Mike Windischmann during a brawling match in which too many players were kicking anything but the ball

Saint reports

This was an ugly, ill-tempered match that was a scar on the World Cup and unworthy of the beautiful setting of Florence. One player was sent off and eight others booked as the game degenerated into a vicious brawl. The football was more out of the Michael Corleone than the Michaelangelo school of soccer.

The Austrians needed a cricket score to keep alive their slim hopes of surviving into the second phase, and when the Americans refused to crumble they resorted, like spoilt children, to petty and sometimes violent fouls. One thing we learned about the Americans is that they can look after themselves in a rough-house, and they gave as good as they got as everything was kicked except the ball.

Syrian referee Jamal Al-Sharif must have felt he had walked into a war zone. It needed more like a sheriff to keep the peace. He sent off Austrian midfield player Peter Artner in the 34th minute for a wicked two-footed tackle, and was brandishing the yellow card so often that he looked like a demented Paul Daniels.

Austria were kept waiting 50 minutes for their first goal. Striker Andreas Ogris ran half the length of the pitch before steering the ball into the net. Twelve minutes later Gerhard Rodax at last made some sort of impact on a tournament that should have been made for a man of his talent when he scored a simple goal from close range.

Just as the Austrians were wondering whether they had done enough to sneak into the second phase the Americans damaged their goal averages when goalkeeper Klaus Lindenberger fumbled a Bruce Murray shot and watched in anguish as it rolled into the net. To be honest, after this shameful display Austria did not deserve a place among the last 16.

Greavsie reports

If Italy can maintain the fire-furnace form they showed against Czechoslovakia in Rome they will not only win the World Cup but do it in a style that would match even the fabulous Brazilian champions of 1970.

They won by two goals to nil, but it could easily have been five or six if the chances they created with such verve and nerve had been converted.

Make no mistake, this is a magnificent Italian team – better than the Dino Zoff side that won the World Cup in 1982, and probably the most adventurous and exciting in their history. They failed to get the anticipated hatful of goals against the United States, but even in that game they played some sparkling soccer that was a joy to this old boy.

While we look on in wonder at their attack, it is worth noting that they are the only team in the tournament to have reached the second phase without conceding a single goal. They are beautifully composed in all departments, and in goalkeeper Walter Zenga have a stylish and dependable last line of defence who has been beaten only twice in his last 13 international appearances. That's some record.

Italy went into this match against a cultured Czech side knowing that a draw would have pushed them down into runners-up place in the group table. That would have meant the Czechs staying in Rome for the second-phase match, while the Italians would have had to travel to Bari. So it was very much in Italy's interests to win, and to stay in Rome where the fanatical support is almost worth a goal start.

Manager Azeglio Vicini decided on a bold change of strike force after Gianluca Vialli had reported a nagging injury. In place of Vialli and Andrea Carnevale he picked "supersub" Salvatore Schillaci and the most expensive footballer on earth, Roberto Baggio, who had been bought by Juventus just a month before the World Cup kicked off for a staggering fee of £8 million.

Within nine minutes Schillaci had signalled his gratitude for being able to start the match by heading in a stormer of a goal after that maestro of a midfield player Giuseppe Giannini (good old Joe Johnson to you and me) had topped an attempted volley. Schillaci met the ball on the rise and powered it past goalkeeper Jan Stejskal.

From then on there was no holding Schillaci. Looking as aggressive as a pit terrier yet silky smooth with the ball at his feet, he ran the Czech defence ragged with a performance that demanded inclusion in all Italy's remaining matches (and on this showing there should be four, including the final). He might have earned two penalties in the second half if he had not made a meal of going down as if trying to earn score tariff points off the diving board. I am sure he was fouled each time, but French referee Joel Quinou gave the Czech defenders the benefit of the doubt because Schillaci exaggerated the effect of the tackles. I thought it was brave (almost foolish) of the ref to turn down both penalty appeals in front of a Roman crowd. There were groans of disappointment from the frenzied Italian spectators as Baggio squandered two chances, and again when Nicola Berti had a shot blocked by overworked goalkeeper Stejskal.

I should not think the Czechs could believe that they were still in the game with a chance of saving it, yet they were desperately unlucky not to be awarded an equaliser in the 67th minute. It seemed a perfectly good goal to me when Stanislav Griga headed the ball into the net after a rare Czech incursion into the Italian goal area. It was ruled off-side much to the relief of Italy. An equaliser at this stage would have been hugely flattering to the Czechs, but they were entitled to feel aggrieved because the way I saw it they had definitely been robbed of a goal.

Italy tried a little robbery of their own when Berti claimed a goal after he had clearly handled the ball, but the referee quite properly ruled out this attempt at a "hand-of-God" goal and booked the offending player.

Then Baggio stepped on to the stage to show

Above: Roberto Baggio on his way to scoring Italy's second goal that Greavsie says was "a masterpiece worthy of an oil painting, let alone a photograph."

Right: Salvatore Schillaci celebrates another goal in World Cup '90. "When I first saw him," says the Saint, "I thought he was a good player. He has forced me to adjust my rating of him. He is a great player."

just why he is he carrying the world's highest price tag. He killed off the Czechs with the goal of the tournament to date, a real masterpiece that was worth an oil painting, let alone a photograph. He expertly exchanged passes with Paolo Maldini, and then tricked his way past two tackles as if the defenders did not exist before planting the ball wide of Stejskal with as classy a finishing shot as you could wish to see. It was a moment to treasure and lifted World Cup '90 to new heights of glory.

 Saint comments

I thought Salvatore Schillaci was a good player when I saw him come on as a substitute in Italy's first two matches. By the end of this classic confrontation with Czechoslovakia I had been forced to adjust my rating of him. He's a *great* player.

There's something almost old-fashioned about him, both in his appearance and in his approach to the game. He does not go in for a modern haircut, and looks almost menacing with what seems a 1950s crew cut. He is short and stocky, and has plenty of spring in his thick thighs. Salvatore is a bit of a tearaway in the style of, say, a Nat Lofthouse, but his ball skills and awareness make him ideal for the contemporary game.

Italy have been keeping him tucked out of sight, awarding him only a handful of caps before the start of Italia '90. But the world should have been aware of his goal-plundering talents because he banged in 15 goals for Juventus last season, which is the equivalent of 30 in the British game where defences are less disciplined. His partnership with the elegant Roberto Baggio could blossom into something really special, both for club and for country, and it will be interesting to watch and see if a place will be found for Gianluca Vialli – a footballing genius who would walk into any other team in the finals.

At this stage the signs are that Italy can all the way to the final in their bid to win the World Cup for a record fourth time. It is going to take either a very special side or a very lucky one to stop them.

QUOTE UNQUOTE

Azeglio Vicini, Italy's manager: "This was the performance I asked for from my players, and they gave me everything they had. It was a pleasure and a privilege to watch them. Baggio's performance was extraordinary for its individual skill and its athletic freshness. He and Schillaci fitted together perfectly, but it is too early to say whether they will start our next match. We must first wait to see exactly who we are playing and weigh up all the factors once we know the position regarding the fitness of all our players. It was important that we should finish at the top of our group because we wanted to continue to play in Rome. It did look as if Czechoslovakia were unlucky to have their goal ruled out, but anybody who saw this match will admit that we should have had at least two more goals. It was an exceptional performance, but we will not get complacent. We know that the real business starts with our next match."

Jozef Venglos, Czechoslovakia's manager: "Italy have a magnificent team, and their performance against us underlines why they are the favourites along with West Germany to win the Cup. I was pleased with our display considering the pressure we were under, and for as long as I live I will never understand why the referee ruled out the goal by Griga. It looked perfect from where I was sitting. Baggio's goal was the real killer. No defence in the world could have prevented that one. It was a brilliant piece of individual skill."

Roberto Baggio, scorer of the wonder goal for Italy: "When the ball went into the net I wanted to kiss everyone in the stadium – every Italian in the world. I hope this clinches a place for me in the team for the next match, but the manager will select what he thinks is the right team for the job. Nobody is looking for personal glory. Everybody in the squad is united as one man to try to win the World Cup for Italy."

Wednesday June 20
Brazil (0) **1**, **Scotland** (0) **0**
Group C, Turin

 Saint reports

Scotland's supporters can swim all the way home from Italy on a sea of tears after seeing their team push the self-destruct button yet again. For the fifth time in as many consecutive appearances in the World Cup finals, Scotland look set for an early departure after this defeat by Brazil that leaves them with only despair to show for all their effort.

We have to wait until the final averages have been worked out at the end of the group matches, but as I prepare these notes for the book I am anticipating the worst. Scotland's survival as one of the third-place teams is too remote a possibility to contemplate, and it would require some freak results in the remaining games.

The goal that signalled Scotland's seemingly certain exit came nine minutes from the end of an unexceptional match in which Brazil were apparently content to coast to a draw. They had done a lot of threatening with rapid passing movements, but they appeared to be almost uninterested in getting involved in any penalty-area skirmishes with a Scottish defence reinforced by the introduction of the same sweeper system that had served England so well against Holland.

It seemed the only way the Brazilians would score was if Scotland gave them a goal, and it chills my Scottish blood to have to report that this is exactly what we did. The nightmare started when Alemao hit a low, speculative shot from 20 yards. The ball bounced and skidded across the wet surface, but goalkeeper Jim Leighton appeared to have it covered. In fairness to Jim, who I am sure will be heavily criticised for what happened next, the ball kicked unkindly at the last moment and what should have been a straightforward save suddenly became fraught with danger. Instead of going into his hands the ball smacked against his chest and upper arms before spinning loose five yards in front of him. Gary Gillespie, on as a substitute for the dazed Murdo MacLeod, was first to react and attempted to clear under pressure from Careca. The ball squirted off to the right where Muller managed to squeeze it into the net from the tightest of angles, while the suddenly immobile Alex McLeish looked on as if the shock of what was happening had turned him to stone.

I felt desperately sorry for Leighton, who was just emerging from his dark tunnel of misery after being dropped from Manchester United's FA Cup Final replay team a month earlier. He had handled with confidence all the way up to the moment when Brazil cobbled their goal out of nothing, and while I would not blame him entirely for the ball finishing in the net I am sure he would accept that nine times out of ten he would have held on to Alemao's shot.

From playing a totally defensive game, Scotland now had to switch to desperate attack. They had created only one real scoring chance before Brazil's goal when David McPherson met a Stuart McCall corner with a downward header that was booted off the goal-line by Branco. Moments before Brazil's shattering goal Robert Fleck had come into the game as substitute for the tiring Ally McCoist, but he was still trying to pick up the pace of the match when it was all over.

Manager Andy Roxburgh had sent Scotland out to play with 11 men behind the ball, and they became disjointed as they tried to go forward in numbers in a panic-propelled hunt for a goal. Brazil looked to be controlling their attempts to claw their way back into the game and into the World Cup with quiet ease, but then in the dying seconds we were given sudden hope of a lifesaver. The ball dropped at the feet of Maurice Johnston six yards from goal, and I was one of 15,000 Scots in the stadium who jumped out of our seats in anticipation of a dramatic equaliser. But then we sank with disappointment as Claudio Taffarel proved why he is considered the greatest Brazilian

Facing page: Murdo MacLeod tries to head the ball towards Brazil's goal in the face of an attempted bicycle kick by Alemao

44

goalkeeper for years by finger-tipping Mo's shot away for a corner-kick.

Johnston fell face first to the turf and lay there as if he had been shot. His reaction captured the utter desolation felt by every Scot in Turin and all those millions watching at home on television.

I had expected Brazil to win, but the manner of their victory was far from glorious. They hardly broke sweat, and I was left wondering just what they are saving for the next phase. So far they have produced little to support my early claims that they would win the World Cup. But they won all three of their group matches, and you get the feeling that they have done it without having to shift out of second gear. It will be intriguing to see what they can achieve when they really put their foot on the accelerator.

I shall now hand over to Greavsie while I go away in a corner and add my tears to all those that have already been shed over the demise of Scotland.

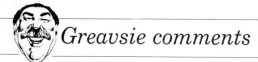

Greavsie comments

Like you, Saint, I felt devastated for poor Jim Leighton. Manchester United manager Alex Ferguson has a lot to answer for. When he left his most loyal of all players out of the FA Cup Final replay team I considered it the cruellest team selection decision of all time. It could only have destroyed the man's self-belief, and even though he earned a vote of confidence from Andy Roxburgh you could sense that he was not far off breaking point.

He will now always be remembered as the man who was dropped from the FA Cup Final and then dropped the ball against Brazil. But having studied the action replay several times I feel Alex McLeish must share the blame for not giving better support. He should have got back to the goal-line to challenge Muller instead of watching like a spectator.

Scotland played a brave defensive game, but I would have admired them more if they had gone for the throat and kept faith with the Fleck–Johnston–Durie combination that sank Sweden.

QUOTE UNQUOTE

Andy Roxburgh, Scotland's manager: "I am obviously disappointed at the cruel way we lost after getting so close to shutting out Brazil. The better side won the game, but to lose a goal in such an unfortunate way is obviously very upsetting. We gave the goal away when players were getting tired, and that is when mistakes are most often made. There are still mathematical possibilities that we will get into the second phase, but our fate is now in the hands of others. All we can do is wait, watch and agonise. I feel so sorry for our supporters. They have been magnificent throughout the tournament, and have been a credit to themselves and to Scotland. I just wish we could have given them a victory against Brazil to celebrate. We created as many, if not more chances than them. Our objective was to try to get a draw, but it was not to be. To say we are disappointed would be an understatement."

Sebastiao Lazaroni, Brazil's manager: "I admired Scotland's performance. They made it very difficult for us, and perhaps deserved a draw. We were a little fortunate with the goal, but football is all about making the most of your chances. We feel we are beginning to get into our rhythm just in time for the important second phase of the tournament. I admit that we have yet to play as well as we can, but we have won all our group matches and that is just the foundation we need on which to build for what we hope will be success in the later stages. Much is expected of us at home in Brazil. We will do our utmost not to let them down and also to give our vast army of travelling supporters something to shout about. Our match against Argentina in the second phase should be, what shall I say, quite interesting!"

Roy Aitken, Scotland's skipper: "We will be roaring England and Ireland on in their next matches. Victories by them could yet clinch a place for us in the second phase."

Roger Flores, skipper of Costa Rica, equalises against Sweden with a glancing header from a floating freekick by Juan Cayasso.

 *Greavsie reports*

Costa Rica have confounded everybody by qualifying for the second phase, and they have emerged along with Cameroon as the most underestimated team in the finals. They came from behind to give sad Sweden their third defeat in this topsy-turvy tournament.

It was an inspired substitution by manager Bora Milutinovic that swung the game Costa Rica's way after Johnny Ekstroem had given Sweden the lead in the 32nd minute when he side-footed in from close range following a well-struck freekick by Stefan Schwarz. The Swedes had been enjoying the better of the game until Milutinovic sent on Hernan Medford on the hour in place of Roger Gomez.

Back home in Costa Rica Medford is idol-ised by the fans for his attacking style but is the despair of coaches because of his inconsistency. He almost scored with his first touch, and then proceeded to run the Swedish defence into dizzy disarray. The Swedes were so rattled by him that they resorted to unconventional methods to try to stop him, and Costa Rica were awarded a free kick in the 75th minute after Medford had been grabbed by the scruff of the neck by Schwarz. Juan Cayasso floated the free kick into the goalmouth and skipper Roger Flores netted with a glancing header.

Sweden, whose exceptional young striker Tomas Brolin had been forced out of the game by some hefty tackling, began to come apart at the seams and, fittingly, it was the dazzling Medford who snatched the winning goal for the Central Americans when he broke through to score with a coolly placed shot in the 87th minute. Eureka Costa Rica!

47

Thursday June 21	Thursday June 21
Belgium (1) **1**, **Spain** (2) **2**	**Uruguay** (0) **1**, **South Korea** (0) **0**
Group E, Verona	Group E, Udine

 Saint reports

 Greavsie reports

Spain are at last mounting the sort of World Cup challenge in keeping with their status as one of Europe's leading footballing nations. They gave a sterile showing against Uruguay in their opening match, outclassed South Korea and then, in this final Group E match, edged to victory over an extremely useful Belgian team.

Both sides had already qualified for the second phase before the kick-off and it would have been understandable if they had been content just to spar for a draw, but they each set their stall out for a victory and provided a contest that was overloaded with quality football. Michel, hat-trick hero against the Koreans, put Spain into the lead in the 26th minute from the penalty spot after Belgian goalkeeper Michel Preud'Homme had pulled down Julio Salinas as he shaped to shoot.

Just three minutes later Belgium were level. Free kicks in this tournament have lacked the imagination and direction of previous finals, but Patrick Vervoort found a way through the Spanish defensive wall with a fierce shot that got a slight deflection on its path into the net.

Spanish international teams of the past might have buckled after this disappointment, but the side pieced together by the former international idol Luis Suarez is made of sterner stuff. With Salinas and Martin Vazquez injecting pace and power, they took command and were well worth their second goal in the 39th minute when defender Alberto Gorriz got up at the far post to head in a free kick fired across from near the left corner flag by Michel.

Spain were content to play a contain-and-counter game in the second half, and at the peak of an intense hunt for a second equaliser Belgium's skilful Enzo Scifo struck a penalty against the bar. Neither Spain nor Belgium look potential World Cup winners, but they will not be easy to eliminate from the race.

Uruguay were just seconds away from elimination from the World Cup when a goal by substitute Daniel Fonseca saved them in a messy, mediocre match against South Korea that did little credit to either team.

From the casual way they played, it was difficult to believe that Uruguay needed to win this game to stay in the tournament. Korea were already out, and a draw would have given Scotland and Austria the opportunity to have taken part in a Russian roulette drawing of lots that might have saved one of them from an early return home.

Even when South Korea were reduced to ten men in the 72nd minute after defender Yoon Deuk-yeo had been sent off for time wasting Uruguay still seemed hardly bothered about pushing forward with any sort of urgency. It was almost as if they had been wrongly advised that a goalless draw would have been enough to clinch a place for them in the second phase.

Fonseca was sent on as a substitute for Ruben Sosa, Uruguay's star striker, who played as if he had lead in his boots. The game was two minutes into injury time when Fonseca finally got the vital goal with a well-directed header from an Alfonso Dominguez free-kick.

It was a bruising battle on a slippery pitch, and as well as sending off Deuk-yoo Italian referee Tullio Lanense booked three Koreans and two Uruguayans. What a sad farewell to the World Cup for a South Korean team that always looked out of its depth and finished with only one goal and no points to show for their endeavours.

Uruguay are a two-faced team. They can play some stunning football, but appeared to be no more than ordinary against South Korea. Even at their best I do not see them being a match for Italy in the second phase.

 Saint reports

Niall Quinn, the truly all-Irish boyo from Dublin, snatched the most important goal in Ireland's football history to send Jack Charlton's Republic team through to the second phase just as it looked as if Holland were going to give them the old heave-ho.

Say what you like about the way Ireland play their blood-and-guts football, but you cannot take away from them the fact that they have tremendous character. For the second time in this tournament they had to come from behind to salvage the game, and this time against a Dutch team playing much more like the side that won the the European Championship two years ago.

Quinn, selected in preference to Tony Cascarino in the only change to the team that drew 0–0 in the unsatisfactory encounter with Egypt, banged in his memorable goal in the 71st minute to cancel out a blinder of a goal by Ruud Gullit. Producing flashes of his best, Gullit knocked the wind out of the Irish in the 10th minute with a goal of pure genius. Running on to a free kick from Ronald Koeman, he exchanged deadly accurate passes with Wim Kieft before racing between two defenders and beating goalkeeper Pat Bonner with a killer of a shot into the far corner of the net.

I feared for Ireland's World Cup life, but they battled back as only they can and their revival movement started to reach a peak when Charlton made a hit-or-bust double substitution in the 62nd minute. Cascarino came on for John Aldridge and Ronnie Whelan, recovered from injury, made his World Cup debut in place of Kevin Sheedy.

Nine minutes after this bold throw of the

Left: Ruud Gullit, the man with the dreadlocks, gets in a tangle as he tries to break the deadlock with a header

49

dice by Charlton and his coach, former England international Maurice Setters, man mountain Quinn scored the goal that will make him a folk hero at home in Ireland.

As with much of Ireland's football, the goal owed little to sophistication and subtlety. The foundation was laid in predictable fashion by a long clearance from goalkeeper Pat Bonner that was meant for the head of Cascarino. The ball bounced free to van Aerle, who for some reason attemped a suicidal back pass to Hans van Breukelen. It was the last thing that the former Nottingham Forest goalkeeper was expecting and he failed to collect the ball, which cannoned off his chest into the path of the alert Quinn. He needed no second invitation to ram it into the net for the most vital goal of his life.

Both teams then came to what seemed an almost mutual agreement to play out the rest of the match for a draw rather than run the risk of a defeat that would have put them on the plane home. Before this cease-fire there were ominous signs that Holland were returning to top form, but Ireland thoroughly deserved their draw and there was another bonus coming their way when the shooting and the shouting were over. Holland and Ireland finished exactly level on points and goals, and a drawing of lots decided that Ireland should be placed second in the group. This meant they had Romania as second round opponents, while the dubious honour for Holland was a match against joint favourites West Germany.

 *Greavsie comments*

Jack O'Charlton was as jumpy as a jack rabbit before this match against Holland, and walked out on a press conference after a blarney barney with footballer-turned-writer Eamonn Dunphy, who had claimed Ireland's performance against Egypt made him ashamed to be Irish. As somebody with a granny called Katie O'Reilly and more than a drop of Irish blood, I could not see what Dunphy was on about. Ireland play to their strengths and don't try to win any prizes for being pretty to watch. They held England and Holland on merit, and will be a handful for Romania in the second phase.

QUOTE UNQUOTE

Ruud Gullit, Holland's goal-scorer: "Everybody should be warned to watch out for Ireland. They are very dangerous. Nobody likes playing against them because they are physically strong and impose themselves on you. I am not being critical of them because I admire what they are achieving, and I honestly believe they can go a long, long way in this tournament. They are very powerful in midfield, and the team has much more to offer than people expected. From my own point of view, I was pleased with my performance against Ireland. I am beginning to feel motivated and am regaining my sharpness with every game. Against West Germany I intend to be completely liberated."

Jack Charlton, Ireland's manager: "I have said all along that the hardest part would be qualifying for the second phase. Now we've done it and nobody should bet against us. I can't believe some of the things that have been written and said about us. I've not enjoyed the World Cup so far. There's been too much hassle and I've found all the hanging around very boring. But hopefully it will get better now."

Mick McCarthy, Ireland's skipper: "Ruud Gullit and I had a quiet word when we scored the equaliser. I'm not telling you what I said, but I don't think the Egyptians would have been too pleased with the way we started to waste time. The referee had a word with me and said why don't we play football. I replied, 'This is the first time we've played football in the whole competition.' All that mattered was getting through to the last 16. This is the greatest day of my life."

Niall Quinn, Ireland's goal hero: "This was my first game at top international level for three years. What a way to come back! All I could think when the scoring chance came my way was, 'Niall, for God's sake don't miss it.'"

Greavsie reports

Mark Wright's first goal in international football catapulted England into the second phase of World Cup '90 and slammed shut the door on an Egyptian team that got the desserts their negative approach deserved.

I have to be honest and say that England did not exactly cover themselves with glory with this victory, but progress to the second round was of paramount importance and of greater concern than the quality of the performance.

Egypt played with just the one ambition of stopping England from scoring, and – as against Ireland – tried to strangle the life out of the game with the sort of aggravating time-wasting tactics that had brought a volley of verbal abuse from Jack Charlton.

Following England's excellent display against Holland I was convinced that Bobby Robson would retain the new sweeper system, but he confounded everybody by reverting to the old flat back four with his loyal servant Terry Butcher being relegated to the touchline bench. Skipper Bryan Robson failed a fitness test on his Achilles tendon injury despite mental massaging from a faith healer. Steve McMahon was given the opportunity to make amends for his error against Ireland, and Steve Bull was brought in as a plundering partner for Gary Lineker, who played after having his badly bruised right big toe frozen with a pain-killing injection.

Egypt's defence was built as solidly as a pyramid, and as hard as England chipped away at it they could make few inroads in a first half during which the midfield was as choked as the M25 in the rush-hour. Paul Gascoigne knitted moments of magic into the frantic, frenzied action but his more experienced partners, John Barnes and Chris Waddle, were again conspicuous by their absence from any

Mark Wright shoulders arms against Egyptian dangerman Hamid Gamal

attacking moves. Full-backs Paul Parker and Stuart Pearce produced more danger down the wings than Barnes and Waddle. Obviously these two gifted but enigmatic players have got to give a lot more to England's cause if they want to come home with any sense of pride.

Significantly, it was the persistent Parker who unleashed England's only genuine shot before half-time after making the sort of right-wing run we had been hoping and expecting to see from Waddle. Even when sweeper Hany Ramzi went off temporarily for treatment to a twisted ankle England could still not break down the Egyptian defence. The anticipated twin thrust from Lineker and Bull just did not happen, and too often they found themselves occupying each other's space.

But at least England were making attempts to win the game. Egypt had two players booked for time-wasting, and their one bid to trouble goalkeeper Peter Shilton in the first half was a ridiculously ambitious shot from all of 35

yards. It would take more than that to beat one of the world's greatest goalkeepers.

England were reduced to ten men when Wright scored his dramatic goal in the 59th minute. Des Walker was lying on the perimeter of the pitch having treatment to a leg injury and looked on anxiously as England were awarded a free kick out near the left touchline half-way into Egypt's half. Gazza placed the ball just a couple of yards from where Walker was lying and floated a high kick tantalisingly into the packed Egyptian penalty area. It hung long enough in the air to tempt goalkeeper Ahmed Shubeir off his line, and he was stranded as the tall figure of Wright rose above all around him. He connected with a glancing header and the ball flicked into the net off defender Hesham Yakan.

England's set-piece play has been superior to much of what we have seen in these finals, and it was clearly going to give them the best chance to pierce Egypt's nine-man defence. It was a marvellous moment for Wright, who has equipped himself exceptionally well since getting his call-up to the World Cup stage.

Shilton, skipper in the absence of Robson and Butcher, earned his corn with an excellent one-handed save when diving to his right to stop a Hamid Abdel shot. England had to carve this vital victory out of pyramid stone.

 Saint comments

After the promise of their exciting performance against Holland I thought England were something of a disappointment against Egypt. The biggest mystery is why John Barnes, who looks a genius at the game when he pulls on a Liverpool shirt, just doesn't seem to be able to function for England. He has *got* to come good in the next match against Belgium or his international future could be in doubt. Egypt lived down to expectations. I cannot understand a team getting to this stage of the World Cup and then playing so negatively.

Facing page: Mark Wright's magical moment as he climbs above the Egyptian defenders to head his first goal for England

QUOTE UNQUOTE

Mark Wright, England's goal hero: "This is the proudest moment of my life. I'm a great patriot, and to score for England in such an important match has made me feel ten feet tall. I should score more goals, but I've made up for all my misses with this one. I only got the merest of touches and I think I must have lost a few strands of hair when the ball brushed my head. I can't believe it's all happening. Just a few weeks ago it was touch and go whether I would make it to Italy because of an injury."

Bobby Robson, England's manager: "We have reached target number one, and that is to get into the last 16. Egypt made it very difficult for us, as they also did for Holland and for the Republic of Ireland. I feel very sorry for them that they have put so much effort into their matches but are having to go home early. We were on a knife edge, and we could not relax until Mark scored that fine goal. We have really worked at our set pieces and this is the reward. Belgium are going to be a hard side to beat, but I'm sure they are not relishing the prospect of playing against us. I have had them watched in all their games and will now make a careful study of the reports. There is a great mood of confidence in our camp, but not a hint of complacency. I'll tell you something – there are six players in our team who are good enough to play for any side and on any stage in the world. I hope they are now going to start getting the praise and the credit that they deserve."

Paul Gascoigne, England's inspirational midfield star: "I'm thoroughly enjoying my first World Cup, but it's all flashing past so quickly that I can hardly take it all in. Now that we're through to the second round I don't think we need be frightened of any country in a one-off situation. The draw has been kind to us, and we are in the mood to try to go all the way."

World Cup chat-a-thon

That's the first phase over, Greavsie. We're now down to the *real* tournament, with just 16 teams left. Would you say that the best 16 teams have qualified for the second round?

I honestly felt sorry for the Soviet Union when they failed to qualify. They looked tremendous when they took Cameroon apart, and they were the victims of a diabolical piece of refereeing in their match with Argentina. Maradona handled the ball right in front of the ref and he didn't see it. A penalty for the Soviets then and it might easily have been Argentina making the early trip home. In their first match they were unlucky to concede a penalty against Romania. Action replays prove that the handling offence happened outside the box. I also felt sorry for you when the poor old Jockos were booked on the early flight out of Italy. But they didn't help themselves with that appalling opening performance against Costa Rica.

I think you're being a little harsh there, Jim. I've studied a recording of that match and do you know that the Scots created no fewer than 19 scoring chances against the Costa Ricans. The footballing gods just weren't smiling on us that day. If there had been any justice we would have won by at least two clear goals against a team that has since proved much better than anybody expected. We must make sure some good comes out of the disappointment of our early exit. The first thing we've got to do is reshape our domestic football so that quality becomes the key word. You can't be totally happy with England's performances.

The only good thing I can say is that at least we have achieved the first objective of reaching the last 16, but only in the match against Holland did we play football of which we could be

"Why is that man called Saint John? He didn't look very saintly to me when Scotland lost."

reasonably proud. We were reduced to kick-and-rush against Jack O'Charlton's Irish battlers, and in the match with Egypt too many of our so-called star players failed to function. For the life of me, I cannot make out Chris Waddle and John Barnes. They are as talented as any footballers produced in Britain over the last 20 years, but so far in this tournament they have made hardly a pin-prick of an impact. It must be sickening for real competitors like David Platt, Neil Webb and Trevor Steven to sit on the touchline bench watching Waddle and Barnes performing without any passion.

England's group was certainly the most miserly. There were only seven goals scored in six matches, compared with 21 in West Germany's group and double figures in all the others. Anyway, you can't read too much into what happens in the first round. Germany in 1954 and 1974 and Argentina in 1978 went on to win the World Cup after losing first-round matches. Which

54

teams have most impressed you, apart from the obvious three favourites Italy, West Germany and Brazil?

 I like the look of Yugoslavia, Czechoslovakia and Romania, and any one of them could cause the more favoured teams a lot of trouble. All of them have a sharpness in attack that has been missing from England's performances. I am also taken by the midfield guile of Belgium. Enzo Scifo, their Italian-born playmaker, looks a top-quality player and could cause England all sorts of problems in their second round match. What do you think of the refereeing, Saint? Don't you think it's been too fussy and inconsistent?

Well the refs have had the yellow card out so many times that the pitches have looked like a field of daffodils. There have so far been a record eight sendings off and more than a hundred bookings. That gives the impression that it has been a violent World Cup, but I've seen heavier tackling in a monastery garden. The refs are clearly under instructions to stamp down on the slightest hint of rough play, but too many of them seem more interested in making sure players are following FIFA rules regarding the wearing of their shirts inside their shorts and that they have their socks pulled up. It's become a big joke.

At least the crowd behaviour has been much better than expectedl. I suppose a lot of that has been due to the ban on alcohol, but I understand the Italian hoteliers and their non-football guests are not exactly pleased. Imagine an American tourist visiting Italy without a clue that there's a big ball game on and finding they can't enjoy a glass of vino with their meal. Mind you, that's preferable to having drunken hooligans smashing up the place.

There was also a lot of discontent among the FIFA football authorities at the way Sardinia was turned almost into a war zone to keep the English and Dutch fans under surveillance. I

A famous Saint & Greavsie fan joins in the World Cup debate

Giller

JUST ONE GOALNETTO WILL DO ITALY

"Oi, Greavsie, wipe that stupid grin orf your face and tell that Maradona geezer to stop falling about. Maradona's more theatrical than Madonna. And as for that Scotch git who works with yer..."

have to admit it left a nasty feeling in the stomach when we had to approach the grounds in Cagliari and Palermo as if we were entering a battleground. There was a feeling among some of the FIFA chiefs that England should be barred from the next World Cup rather than have to resort to putting any ground where they play on a war footing. What do you think of that?

I'm as much against hooligans as anybody, but it would be blind and foolish to see it purely as an English problem. If they ban England they would surely also have to kick out West Germany and Holland, who have as big if not a worse hooligan problem than us. And the Italians are not exactly squeaky clean. The story I've heard from Sardinia is that the few outbreaks of violence were caused by local yobs starting on our supporters. I hate the idea of grounds being ringed with armed police, but if that is what has to be done to keep the peace then so be it. Rather that than give in to the minority of mindless idiots who go to football purely for kicks of the worst kind.

Scotland's fans can be excluded from all you're saying. I saw them behaving impeccably before, during and after the match with Brazil. They were a credit to Scotland, and if any supporters deserved to have a team in the second phase it

55

was them. What I will say, Jim, is that it's a wonder some of the players have not caused violent crowd reaction with their play-acting.

That's been the worst feature of an otherwise satisfactory tournament to date. As I've said before, the professional *fall* is as big a scar on the game as the professional *foul*. I have to say that the South Americans have been the worst culprits, particularly Colombia and Argentina. Anyway, let's stop dodging the issue. The time has come to select the teams we think will win through to the quarter-finals. The drawback with writing instant opinions like these is that by the end of the book you can look a right Charlie. That's commonplace for me. I'll kick off by predicting that Colombia will beat Cameroon. The Soviets exposed just how naive the Africans are when it comes to defensive tactics, and I think skilful players like Valderrama and Fajardo will pull them inside out. Cameroon have brought great joy and the wonderful element of surprise to these finals, but I think we'll soon be saying *arrivederci* to them.

I'll go along with you there, Greavsie, but Cameroon – and Egypt – have shown such astonishing improvement that I think the day is not too far away when we will see an African country winning the World Cup. Costa Rica have been nearly as big a surprise package as Cameroon, but I think they will be outgunned by Czechoslovakia. They will not let them off the hook like Scotland did.

Agreed. The Czechs are definitely a good outside bet. Brazil against Argentina is a really tough one to predict. Form goes out of the window and emotions take over when these two bitter rivals play. I think Brazil are the better side, but I have a sneaking feeling that the moody Maradona might come out of his deep sleep and cause an upset. He is due to produce one of his memorable performances, and it's now or never for Diego. I suppose you've got to stick with Brazil, as you've picked them to win the World Cup.

Aye, Jim, but I don't feel all that confident. Brazil have been playing in second gear so far, and I just hope they can put it all together when they put their foot down on the accelerator. For the sake of the tournament I hope Brazil win because I think they are the more colourful and enterprising team. Argentina have so far been just a shadow of the side that won the World Cup four years ago, but like you say, Maradona could be waiting to explode.

Then it's the turn of my tip for the Cup, West Germany, to take on Holland. They are almost as bitter with their rivalry as Brazil and Uruguay. There were definite signs that the Dutch were beginning to find their rhythm against Ireland, particularly Ruud Gullit. Even so, I cannot see that they will improve sufficiently to stop the march of Franz Beckenbauer's team.

It will be fascinating to see the battle for supremacy betwen the number tens, Gullit and Lothar Matthaeus. Germany have looked a lot sharper, but have they peaked too early? I shall be going to Genoa to see Ireland take on Romania. That's going to be a tough one for Jack Charlton's boys, but I think they could just squeeze a victory, particularly as the Romanians will be without the suspended Lacatus.

I hope you're proved right, Saint, but the Romanians are a very tasty side if given the room in which to play. I reckon Jack's plan will be to stop them getting into any sort of playing pattern. I tipped Yugoslavia as outsiders for the Cup before a ball was kicked, and I think they'll have too much flair for a Spanish side that has been leaning very heavily on Michel.

Well I take Spain to win. Obviously we're both going for Italy to beat Uruguay, and I know we're agreed that England should conquer the Belgians, but they're a lively and skilful side and England will need to be at the top of their form to master them. All right, Greavsie. That's enough of the pontificating. Now on with the action.

56

World Cup '90: Phase 2

The 16 survivors, and how they line up in the battles for quarter-final places:

June 23, Naples:

Cameroon   v   Colombia

P 3 W 2 D 0 L 1 F 3 A 5 Pts 4   P 3 W 1 D 1 L 1 F 3 A 2 Pts 3

June 23, Bari:

Czechoslovakia   v   Costa Rica

P 3 W 2 D 0 L 1 F 6 A 3 Pts 4   P 3 W 2 D 0 L 1 F 3 A 2 Pts 4

June 24, Turin:

Brazil   v   Argentina

P 3 W 3 D 0 L 0 F 4 A 1 Pts 6   P 3 W 1 D 1 L 1 F 3 A 2 Pts 3

June 24, Milan:

West Germany   v   Holland

P 3 W 2 D 1 L 0 F 10 A 3 Pts 5   P 3 W 0 D 3 L 0 F 2 A 2 Pts 3

June 25, Genoa:

Republic of Ireland   v   Romania

P 3 W 0 D 3 L 0 F 2 A 2 Pts 3   P 3 W 1 D 1 L 1 F 4 A 3 Pts 3

June 25, Rome:

Italy   v   Uruguay

P 3 W 3 D 0 L 0 F 4 A 0 Pts 6   P 3 W 1 D 1 L 1 F 2 A 3 Pts 3

June 26, Verona:

Spain   v   Yugoslavia

P 3 W 2 D 1 L 0 F 5 A 2 Pts 5   P 3 W 2 D 0 L 1 F 6 A 5 Pts 4

June 26, Bologna:

England   v   Belgium

P 3 W 1 D 2 L 0 F 2 A 1 Pts 4   P 3 W 2 D 0 L 1 F 6 A 3 Pts 4

Saturday June 23   Phase 2
Cameroon (0) **2**, **Colombia** (0) **1**
Naples   *(after extra time)*

Two of the most unforgettable characters of Italia '90 come together in one of the most bizarre of all the incidents as Roger Milla dispossesses goalkeeper Rene Higuita before scoring for Cameroon

 Saint reports

Cameroon continue to cause the biggest shocks of World Cup '90, and they have also come up with the unlikeliest hero in the shape of 38-year-old twice-retired international striker Roger Milla. He followed his two goals during his substitute appearance against Romania with two extra-time goals against Colombia after coming off the touchline bench to flourish his ancient yet handsome skills.

The celebrations by Cameroon at getting through to the quarter-final for a showdown against the winners of the England–Belgium match were restricted by the knowledge that four of their players would be missing because of double bookings. Cameroon have mixed the big boot with their subtle approach play, as is revealed by qualifying–group statistics that show they committed more fouls (75) than any other team apart from South Korea (88). They notched up another 39 fouls against Colombia, but few were of the vicious variety, more of the spoiling, needling type that got the Colombians nicely rattled.

I was surprised by Colombia's cautious approach to the match. The Soviets proved that the African defence was suspect under pressure, but they elected to play five men in midfield and just Carlos Estrada up front as a lone hunter for goals. He was unlucky not to be awarded a penalty in Colombia's best move of the first half after 20 minutes when he was hacked down by Stephen Tataw as he raced on to a superb defence-splitting pass from skipper Valderrama.

In the doll-haired Valderrama Colombia

had one of the tournament's most striking characters, but his performance in this most vital game of his career was a disappointment. He played far too deep and was unable to stamp any sort of authority on the match.

Colombia had the better of the first hour of play and were within inches of taking the lead when a Freddy Rincon free kick hit the bar. But Cameroon stayed nicely organised and suddenly began to look capable of moving up a gear when the vastly experienced Milla came on as substitute in the 54th minute.

A tight, tense game came alight in the second period of extra time just as it was looking as if it would take penalties to decide the winners. Milla, a gap-toothed old lion of a campaigner, pounced on a neat, angled pass from Omam Biyick in the 107th minute, raced past two defenders, hurdled an attempted tackle and then steered a left-footed shot past oncoming goalkeeper Rene Higuita.

Milla's second goal three minutes later was a gift from the wildy eccentric Higuita. He was playing his crazy sweeper role miles outside his penalty area when he lost the ball to Milla while trying to exchange passes. Milla raced 30 yards before shooting into an empty net.

Colombia pulled a goal back through Bernado Redin with three minutes to go, but Cameroon stayed calm en route to the promised land of the quarter-finals.

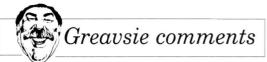 *Greavsie comments*

I was over the moon for Cameroon! What a magnificent feat to have reached the last eight. Nobody gave them a hope before the finals started, yet they have brought not only spirit and style to the tournament but also hope for all those other so-called third-world countries who can now think realistically of one day joining in the greatest soccer show on earth.

Colombia will be kicking themselves for not having sewn up the match in the first hour when they looked the more accomplished side. Then Roger Milla came on to add another chapter to his World Cup '90 fairytale. Make no mistake, Cameroon will certainly not be easy to conquer in the quarter-finals.

Roger Milla, Cameroon's two-goal hero: "I am frightened somebody is going to wake me up and tell me that I am having a sweet dream. Our confidence is growing by the minute, and we now feel deep down that as we have got this far we could even go all the way to the final. Why not? We have beaten the reigning world champions, Romania and now Colombia. This is not luck. We have earned the right to be in the quarter-finals, and we will have no fear of either England or Belgium. It is they who will be worried about us. I had made up my mind to retire from club football, but now I am thinking of a comeback, perhaps in Italy or Spain. I am waiting to listen to any offers. I have never made much money out of football. Maybe now is the time to get something in the bank."

Francisco Maturana, Colombia's manager: "We had our chances to win the game long before extra time, but sadly we did not take them. Our best wishes go to Cameroon. They are a more professional and organised side than anybody expected. Don't write them off in the quarter-finals. They could yet cause more surprises. It was a bad mistake by Higuita that gave them their second goal, but football is human and it is human to err. It will help Higuita grow into a better goalkeeper. He is only 23, and will benefit from this experience."

Rene Higuita, Colombia's eccentric and engaging goalkeeper who is hoping to land a contract with a European club: "That was a big mistake I made. It was as big as a house. Always I play like this. I see myself as a sweeper as well as a goalkeeper. There have been no recriminations from my team-mates. They know the way I play. Today I hold my hands up and admit that I made a mistake. I have asked to be forgiven. I will not change the way I play, but this will not happen again. It will make me a better goalkeeper, you wait and see."

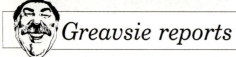 *Greavsie reports*

Tomas Skuhravy, Czechoslovakia's head man, beats two Costa Rican defenders to the ball on his way to a headed hat-trick

Costa Rica's brave challenge crumbled in the face of Czechoslovakia's powerful attack. The glory went to the head of Sparta Prague striker Tomas Skuhravy, who netted a hat-trick of headers. He had the ball in the net a fourth time with his head, but the goal was disallowed.

It was the moment of truth for Costa Rica, who had been reaching above themselves throughout the finals, but they went out of the tournament with their chests inflated with pride. The scoreline flattered Czechoslovakia, who looked no more than two goals the better side.

For the Costa Ricans there was the consolation of knowing they had acquitted themselves far better than anybody expected, and they had two fine wins over Sweden and Scotland to show for all their effort in what was their first appearance in the World Cup finals.

Costa stand-in goalkeeper Hermidio Barrantes played magnificently during a first half when non-stop pressure from Czechoslovakia brought the reward of only one goal. Skuhravy, playing like an old-style centre-forward, climbed impressively to head the first of his goals in the 11th minute following a strong dribble out on the right by Lubomir Moravcik.

Barrantes prevented the Czechs from making it 2–0 just moments later when Ivo Knoflicek raced on to a 60-yard pass and cut in on goal. He tried to lob the ball over the advancing goalkeeper, who threw himself backwards to make a spectacular catch.

There was a spell in the second half when Costa threatened to take command of the game, and their persistence paid off in the 55th minute when Ronald Gonzalez scored a goal out of the Skuhravy book with a powerful header from a curling free kick by Oscar Ramirez. The pendulum of play had swung Costa's way, but as they pressed forward inviting holes were beginning to show at the back of their defence. Skuhravy revealed that he was brave as well as talented in the 62nd minute when he dived full-length to head home in the face of an intended overhead kick clearance.

The Costa Rican defenders had no idea how to control the aerial bombardment from Skuhravy, and Czechoslovakia fed him with a procession of crosses that continually caused consternation in the penalty area.

It was Lubos Kubik who collected the third goal, and in many ways it was the best of the lot. He curled in a classic free kick that swung into the Costa Rican net in the 75th minute. Set-piece play has been disappointing so far in World Cup '90, and it was refreshing to see a free kick taken with skill and power. The

60

South Americans have traditionally led the way in unwrapping inventive free kicks, but there does not seem to have been the same amount of preparation gone into the plotting of set-piece play for these finals. England appear to have put in more thought than most in how to deceive defences with cleverly contrived free kick ploys.

Skuhravy, tall and as strong as a bull, completed his hat-trick against Costa Rica in the 82nd minute with yet another well-directed header. It was his fifth goal of the tournament, and he played with the confidence of a man who feels he has still more goals to come.

This was a solid rather than spectacular performance by the Czechs. The difference between the two teams was purely the power in the air of Skuhravy. He could prove a handful in the quarter-finals.

 ## *Saint comments*

Skuhravy has made no secret of the fact that he would like to play in England, and there should be a stampede of managers to try to sign a player who is like a throwback to the British centre-forwards of the 1950s. His bustling, bulldozing style of play would be ideally suited to the English league, but even as I write I hear on the grapevine that a representative for the Italian club, Genoa, is moving in on Skuhravy with a lorryful of lira.

The Czechs are an impressive side when they are striking forward, but there are question marks about their defence. There seems a lack of real mobility at the back, and there were several occasions when the nippy Costa Ricans got beyond the back markers but without being able to put the vital finishing touch. I would fancy the skilled West Germans or a Dutch master like Ruud Gullit to dismantle the Czech defence. We shall see in the quarter-final in Milan.

Taking up the point that Greavsie makes about free kicks, we are seeing nobody in the class of Rivelino, Garrincha, Cubillas and Michel Platini as dead ball specialists. I am surprised that more care and attention is not being given to this crucial area of the game.

Tomas Skuhravy, Czechoslovakia's hat-trick hero: "This is the greatest day of my life. Who could wish for more than a hat-trick in a World Cup match? But I must not get carried away. The important thing is to try to score more goals in our quarter-final match. I have always prided myself on my heading ability, but I shoot most of my goals. It is my hope that when the World Cup is over I shall be able to play in a major league, perhaps in England. They now know what I have to offer. I have a great admiration for English football. It is played with strength as well as skill, and that is the way I try to play the game."

Jozef Venglos, Czechoslovakia's manager: "Costa Rica made it much more difficult for us than the scoreline indicates. They have great discipline in defence and it was only our supremacy when the ball was in the air that gave us the edge. We are glad to have got this game behind us because the Costa Ricans have proved that they have the ability to beat the very best teams. Now we look forward to the quarter-final match against either West Germany or Holland. They are both giants of football, but I think we could give either of them a lot to think about if we play to the peak of our form. We are very happy with the way things have gone, but all is put into perspective when you hear about terrible tragedies like the earthquake in Iran. It should remind us that football is, at the end of the day, only a game. We shall do our bit to help the Iranians by playing a match against a local side here in Italy, with the proceeds to go to the earthquake fund."

Bora Milutinovic, Costa Rica's manager: "The players are all heroes at home in Costa Rica. They have played with great pride and purpose. I thought we were unlucky to lose by such a margin. But we have no complaints. It has been a wonderful World Cup for us."

Saint reports

Diego Maradona stirred awake like a giant coming out of a deep slumber to bury Brazil with a moment of magic that revealed he is not yet ready to vacate the throne as the modern king of world football. He turned upside down a game that Brazil had totally dominated with the sort of flowing, spontaneous play that made them a joy to watch, and all neutral fans will have mourned their exit against an Argentinian side that can count itself lucky still to have an interest in the tournament.

Brazil could and should have been two or three goals clear before Maradona created Argentina's winner out of nowhere in the 80th minute. Up until then he had been an almost anonymous, sad-looking figure who seemed more interested in whingeing and whining than getting on with trying to turn the tide of attacks that were coming from Brazil in huge waves of brilliance.

Dunga and Alemao were in complete command in midfield, and everything flowed from them. I counted more than half a dozen occasions in the first half when Argentina's defence was turned inside out. All that was missing was the all-important finishing touch. If they'd had a Pelé in attack they would have had a bundle of goals, but that of course is a thought for dreamers. In reality Brazil produced some of the finest football they have displayed since the golden days of the 1970 world champions, but that golden touch turned to stone in front of goal.

Careca, Muller, Valdo and Rocha all made and missed chances before Dunga sent a header thumping against a post. In the second half Muller and Alemao had shots turned against

Facing page: Claudio Caniggia celebrates his goal for Argentina that silenced the drums and broke millions of Brazilian hearts

the woodwork by heavily employed goalkeeper Sergio Goycochea.

Argentina looked like pupils against masters, and they resorted to rugged methods to try to put a brake on Brazil. Monzon and Giusti were both booked for brutal tackles as the world champions clung on by their fingertips to the Cup they won in such style four years ago. Yet after a rush hour of magnificent football from Brazil the game was still goalless, and slowly you could see the Argentinians beginning to grow in confidence. Brazil had rocked them back on their heels a dozen times but without applying the knock-out punch.

The Brazilians, whose cautious tactics in their three group matches had brought roars of disapproval from critics led by the one and only Pelé, had answered the calls for attacking play. But as the game went into its last third without the inspiration of a goal they were suddenly looking nervous. I sensed they were mentally preparing themselves for extra–time when Maradona cut them off at the legs.

For the first time in the tournament he conjured up memories of his marvellous one-man show in Mexico in 1986 as he collected the ball in the half-way circle and then started to accelerate through the yellow curtain of Brazilian players surrounding him. Three defenders queued ahead of him, forcing him on to his right foot. While they were preoccupied with trying to halt Maradona's progress, Caniggia – a blond bombshell of a sprinter – was speeding into the open spaces left by the players drawn to Diego like flies into a spider's web. As he drifted to his right Maradona flicked a perfect pass through the legs of his chasing opponents, and the ball came clean and invitingly into the path of Caniggia, who gave the Brazilians a lesson in finishing. The man who plays his club football in Italy with Atlanta enticed goalkeeper Taffarel off his line and then shot low and true into the empty net for a goal that silenced the banging drums and stopped the sambas of the thousands of Brazilians who had turned the Turin stadium into a meadow of yellow. Suddenly it was mellow yellow.

Moments later Maradona proved that he was well and truly awake when he unleashed a swerving left-footed free kick with all his old venom, and Taffarel had to perform acrobatics

63

to keep it out of the Brazilian net. Diego did a little PR for himself by applauding the save. After his dark moods so far in these finals he needs all the friends he can get.

It was almost beyond belief that Brazil were now struggling to get back into a match they had been monopolising with what was apparent ease. Their desperation was reflected in the reckless tackle that led to a sending-off for skipper Ricardo Gomes after he had sent Jose Basualdo tumbling. In the final minute Muller, named after the great West German goal master Gerd Muller, had a clear chance to snatch an equaliser. He failed to live up to his name, and millions of Brazilian hearts were broken as he sliced his shot into the side netting.

I have thought from the early stages that Maradona has been carrying an injury, and this was confirmed after the match when it was revealed that he needed five pain-killing injections for a damaged ankle that has been hindering him. This miracle win over Brazil will be the best healing treatment for the wee master, and he may yet have a prominent part to play in these astonishing finals.

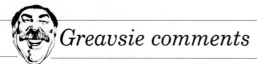 *Greavsie comments*

Football's a cruel old game. Brazil ran Argentina ragged with some of the best football we've seen in World Cup '90, but all they've got to show for their effort is a premature return home. The tournament is a lot poorer for the departure of Brazil, but they have only themselves to blame. It's all about putting the ball in the net, and the Brazilian forwards were guilty of some abysmal finishing.

What is there left to say about 'orrible old Diego? Just as he was looking ready to be buried, he climbed off his death bed and gave us a glimpse of the form that has twice encouraged clubs to pay world record transfer fees for his talent. I don't think any other player in the world could have laid on that chance for Caniggia when surrounded by so many defenders. He not only outwitted three players during his run but lured another three out of position. It was a touch of genius.

QUOTE UNQUOTE

Carlos Bilardo, Argentina's manager: "There are few others players here who would have played in Diego's condition. He has been fouled continually throughout the tournament, and has been troubled by injuries caused by the many kicks he has had to endure. He was unable to train properly, and at half-time we had to give him five pain-killing injections to ease his injured ankle. I asked him to play even though I knew he was not 100 per cent fit – and he played because he is Maradona. He produced the moment we have all been waiting for. No other player could have done it. You have to understand what beating Brazil means to Argentinians. They are our number one rivals, and we have never beaten them in the World Cup. This was like a final for us, and the victory has lifted our morale to the skies."

Diego Maradona, Argentina's goal-maker: "Even though I am not fit I shall play on regardless. Right now my ankle and my knee hurt but I don't care. The sweetness of victory takes away the pain. I just want to enjoy this moment and I know I will be in better shape for the next match. Beating a great team like Brazil will give us greater strength to do well in the competition. I feel deep down that we can match any of the teams that are left. Our confidence has been a little low, but now we are back in the mood of 1986. Whichever way you want to paint the picture, this is an alert to the rest of the world. Argentina are by no means dead, and when we're alive we are very, very dangerous."

Sebastiao Lazaroni, Brazil's manager who was being angrily blamed at home for their exit because of his leaning towards defensive tactics: "It was frustrating to see us making and then wasting so many chances. I felt as if the gods were against us. To me, Maradona is still the player of the day and the way he created their goal was the work of a master."

Saint and Greavsie's TIME MACHINE

WRITTEN AND ILLUSTRATED BY BARRY ROBERTS

THAT'S IT FOR ANOTHER YEAR, JIM. SEE YOU NEXT SEASON.

YEH.. I'LL WRITE NEXT YEAR'S SCRIPTS ON THE WORD PROCESSOR DICKIE DAVIES LOANED ME. I MIGHT EVEN WRITE ANOTHER BOOK. THIS TIME ON FLY FISHING.

FORGET IT. J.R. HARTLEY'S BEATEN YOU TO IT. DO YOU FANCY THAT SATELLITE T.V.?

THERE'S NO WAY YOU'D GET ME UP IN ONE OF THOSE THINGS. THIS MUST BE THE ROOM DICKIE MEANT. I WONDER WHAT SCI-FI MEANS?

SCI-FI DEPT

YOU SURE THIS IS THE RIGHT ROOM? THAT THING DOESN'T LOOK LIKE A WORD PROCESSOR TO ME!

AND HOW WOULD A JOCK KNOW? THEY'RE STILL USING SLATE AND CHALK UP IN JOCKOLAND. OLD DICKIE LIKES HIS COMFORT. IT'S EVEN GOT TWO SEATS. HOP IN.

THIS DIAL'S GOT A DATE ON IT. 1890.

MUST BE TO REMIND DICKIE OF HIS BIRTH-DAY. OR THE LAST TIME THE FA MADE A DECISION. LET'S TRY THIS BUTTON.

WHOOP! WHOOP! WHOOP!

THEY LAND BACK IN 1890

JIM! WE'VE GONE BACK 100 YEARS!

I WAS RIGHT. IT IS SOMETHING TO DO WITH THE FA. LET'S GET OVER TO SPURS. WE MIGHT SEE JIMMY HILL MAKING HIS DEBUT FOR THEM!

IF WE CAN GO BACK 100 YEARS, SAINT.. WE MUST BE ABLE TO GO FORWARD BY JUST ONE WEEK.

WHAT'LL WE LEARN BY JUST A WEEK?

THE POOLS SCORE DRAWS! LET'S GET MOVING. I CAN'T STAND IT HERE. BEER A PENNY A PINT AND I'VE NOT TOUCHED A DROP FOR YEARS!!

1938 WORLD CUP. FRANCE

THIS IS THE YEAR OF THE DICTATOR, JIM. THAT'S HIM UP THERE

HE LOOKS NOTHING LIKE OUR PRODUCER!

HEIL HITLER

NO JIM! REMEMBER.. WE SHALL FIGHT THEM ON THE LAND. WE SHALL FIGHT THEM ON THE BEACHES.

AND ANYWHERE ELSE LEEDS UNITED ARE PLAYING AWAY. SO THIS IS THE WORLD CUP THAT ENDED IN A WAR.

ALL WORLD CUPS END IN A WAR IF URUGUAY ARE PLAYING! LET'S GO.

HALT SVINEHUNT! YOU CAN'T DRIVE ZAT IN HERE!

BLIMEY! QUICK SAINT. IT'S THE L.W.T. CAR PARK ATTENDANT.

THEY ZOOM INTO THE FUTURE. THE YEAR 2020. A BETTER FUTURE. A FUTURE WITHOUT ARCHAIC STADIUMS. HOOLIGANS. AND DES LYNHAM!

ANY CHANGE OVER THE PAST 30 YEARS JIM?

NO. UNITED STILL HAVEN'T WON THE LEAGUE.

I'LL TELL YOU SOMETHING... FRANK BRUNO'S DONE WELL SINCE HIS PANTOMIMES. FANCY HIM BEING AT THE ROYAL SHAKESPEARE COMPANY PLAYING OTHELLO! IS OUR SHOW STILL ON?

LET'S SEE. SATURDAY.. ONE O' CLOCK? SAYS HERE IT'S THE VINNY AND GAZZA SHOW! BLIMEY! LOOK AT THIS PHOTOGRAPH. GAZZA'S ABOUT 16 STONE!

SO HE DID MANAGE TO LOSE WEIGHT! THIS YEAR'S WORLD CUP FINAL LOOKS GOOD. TUNISIA VERSUS THE CAMEROONS! FANCY A LOOK AT LIVERPOOL?

THEY HEAD NORTH TO THE LAND OF A THOUSAND CONES.

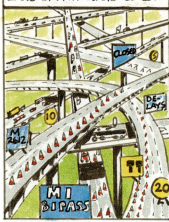

3 DAYS LATER THEY ARRIVE BACK AT WEMBLEY.

HOW WERE WE TO KNOW THIS WAS THEIR HOME GROUND!

I SEE WE'VE STILL GOT PROBLEMS. I WONDER WHAT THAT HOOLIE MACHINE DOES

HERE WE GO! HERE WE GO! HERE WE GO!

GOTCHA!

HOOLI-MACHU

REJECT!

BOOM

INSIDE

A SLIDING ROOF AT WEMBLEY SAINT! THINGS HAVE CHANGED AROUND HERE!

SOME THINGS NEVER CHANGE, JIM. LOOK.

MANAGER

K. DALGLISH

STRICTLY NO INTERVIEWS

HERE'S TODAYS TEAM SHEET. SULIMAN IN GOAL. SCHMIDT, LOPEZ, JONGBLOED, YASHIN, CALOTTI,.. BLIMEY! RONNIE ROSENTHALL STARTED SOMETHING WHEN HE SCORED THAT FIRST GOAL BACK IN 1990!

TEAM
SULIMAN
SCHMIDT
LOPEZ
JONGBLOED
YASHIN
CALOTTI
CHADTZ

MAKE WAY FOR THE SATELLITE T.V. COMMENTATOR

LOOK SAINT. IT'S BRIAN MOORE! YOU CAN'T KEEP AN OLD DOG DOWN.

HOW DO YOU FANCY RE-VISITING THE 1966 WORLD CUP FINAL?

IT WON'T BE THE SAME WATCHING IT FROM A SEAT.

WHY NOT? I WATCHED IT FROM A SEAT THEN! REMEMBER

WE'LL STOP OFF ON THE WAY, SAINT.

WHERE AT?

MEXICO 1986. THERE'S SOMETHING I'VE ALWAYS WANTED TO DO. 22ND OF JUNE IF MY MEMORY SERVES ME WELL.

MEXICO 1986

PSSST. SHILTS.

GREAVSIE! WHAT ARE YOU DOING HERE?

ANY MINUTE NOW, MARADONA IS GOING TO SAIL THROUGH THE AIR AND BANG THE BALL IN WITH HIS FIST. MAKE SURE YOU GET TO HIM FIRST.

THE BALL COMES OVER. MARADONA LEAPS.. BUT SHILTON GETS THERE FIRST.

NEVER MIND THE HAND OF GOD, SAINT. LOOK AT THE FIST OF SHILTS!

SMACK

ANOTHER GOOD IDEA, GREAVSIE!

HE DIDN'T GET HIS HAND TO THE BALL THOUGH.

NO. SHILTS GOT HIS HAND TO HIS NOSE! THE REF GAVE A PENALTY AND YOU STILL LOST 2-1. YOU CAN'T ALTER HISTORY. DIAL 1966.

THEY LAND IN 1966.

WELL JIM. CUP FINAL. MORNING. ALL WE NEED IS A TICKET.

EASY SAINT. I WAS IN THE SQUAD, REMEMBER. SO THEY'RE BOUND TO LET US IN.

AT THE GATE

OI! YOU CAN'T GO IN THERE WITHOUT A TICKET.

BUT I'M JIMMY GREAVES!

ADULTS 17/6⁰

YOU! JIMMY GREAVES! DON'T MAKE ME LAUGH. I KNOW JIMMY GREAVES AND HE'S SLIM, ATH-LETIC. AND HE'S GOT HAIR. NOW PUSH OFF FATSO.

YOU WERE SAYING JIM?

I DON'T THINK I'VE CHANGED ALL THAT MUCH.

BUT I KNOW IAN ST JOHN WHEN I SEE HIM. BE MY GUEST SAINT. AND TAKE HIM WITH YOU. JIMMY GREAVES INDEED.. HA!

HANG ABOUT SAINT. IT'S JACK CHARLTON.

HELLO SAINT YOU MUST HAVE HAD A GOOD TIME LAST NIGHT. YOU LOOK LIKE YOU'VE PUT 20 YEARS ON!

HEY JACK. DON'T WORRY IF YOU HIT THE BAR TODAY.. THEY ALL COUNT!

WHO DO YOU THINK YOU ARE? JIMMY GREAVES? IT'S TIME I GOT BACK TO THE DRESSING ROOM AND HELPED NOBBY STILES LOOK FOR HIS CONTACT LENSES! I HOPE BOBBY MOORE'S HAIRDRESSER HAS FINISHED.

MAKES YOU WONDER WHAT WE DID WITHOUT ACTION REPLAYS AND PANELS, SAINT.

WE SAT BACK AND WATCHED FOOTBALL.

THE COMMENTATOR SHOUTS.

AND PEOPLE ARE ON THE PITCH! THEY THINK IT'S ALL OVER...

WHAM

IT IS NOW!!

THE LIKES OF WHICH WE'LL NEVER SEE AGAIN, SAINT.

Y'NEAN ENGLAND WINNING THE WORLD CUP?

NO.. I MEAN THE FANS CHEERING THE MANAGER.

RAMSEY RAMSEY

LOOK JIM. IT'S YOU!

HEY GREAVSIE! DON'T WORRY ABOUT MISSING THE FINAL. ONE DAY YOU'LL BE A T.V. SUPERSTAR.

HUH! THERE'S AS MUCH CHANCE OF THAT AS BOBBY ROBSON BECOMING THE ENGLAND MANAGER!

LET'S GET BACK TO NORMAL, SAINT. THESE GOOD OLD DAYS ARE MAKING ME FEEL BAD.

ITALY 1990 JIM. WE WERE BOTH HERE AND THE REST IS HISTORY.

YEH. ONLY NOW WE'RE BOTH RICH MEN.

RICH! US?

REMEMBER WHEN I NIPPED INTO KENNY DALGLISH'S OFFICE IN THE YEAR 2020? WELL, I HAD A QUICK LOOK AT THE ROTHMANS YEAR BOOK AND PUT 500 QUID ON THE WINNER! IT SHOULD BE ME WHO'S THE JOCK!

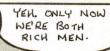

THE END

Greavsie reports

There have been a lot of good games played so far in World Cup '90. This was the first of the great ones, even though it was scarred with some needless violence and a disgraceful spitting incident that brought shame on Holland's exceptional defender Frank Rijkaard. West Germany won a belter of a match on merit, and they continue to carry my confidence that we are seeing the eventual winners of the title.

Let me first of all get the game's one really unsavoury incident out of the way before I start describing the many good things. Rijkaard and German striker Rudi Voeller came into the match clearly with a score to settle from a previous encounter because they were snapping at each other from the first moments of the match. Their two-man war reached its peak, or I should say depths, in the 21st minute when the referee ordered them both off after an angry tangle. I thought Voeller unlucky to be invited to take an early bath because he had every reason to erupt after Rijkaard had twice spat at him. As an ex-pro, let me assure you that inside the game this is considered the greatest of all sins. Kick a pro and he'll usually accept it as part and parcel of the game. Spit at him and you'll turn him into a raging bull.

It was not only a despicable thing for one pro to do to another, but also an appalling example to the millions of youngsters watching the match on worldwide television. Rijkaard deserved a three-month ban for the damage that he did to the image of the game with his gutter-level behaviour.

The game could easily have died on its feet when both sides were reduced to ten men, but not a bit of it. Each team made the most of the extra space left by the departures of Rijkaard and Voeller, and they went flat out at each other like two boxers refusing to give an inch,

and first one team and then the other was left hanging on the ropes.

It was Holland who made the early running against a West German defence that lacked the discipline and control shown in the group matches. Aron Winter, drafted into the Dutch midfield, made two early breaks to get on the end of crosses from Ruud Gullit and then van't Schip. Goalkeeper Bodo Ilgner turned his first effort away for a corner, and with his second shot he grazed the crossbar.

There was a titanic tussle developing for control of the midfield, with Gullit and Lothar Matthaeus parading their skills with thoroughbred style. Like Brazil, Holland will reflect with aching hearts on a string of missed chances. Gullit and the completely subdued Marco van Basten were the biggest culprits.

It was like a home match for Dutch trio Gullit, van Basten and Rijkaard and also Matthaeus, Andreas Brehme and Juergen Klinsmann, all of whom play for the rival AC and Inter Milan clubs at the San Siro stadium.

Klinsmann was the player who looked most at home, and was my choice as man of the match. He played with the fire and fury of two men following the dismissal of his plundering partner Voeller. Here, there and everywhere, he worried and hurried the Dutch defenders into making mistakes and was too quick for them six minutes after half-time when he nipped in between Jan Wouters and Ronald Koeman to flick a low cross from Guido Buchwald deftly into the net from close range.

It was a classical striker's goal, and he almost added a second in the 75th minute with a thundering shot against the post after a storming run through the Dutch defence. Klinsmann had just about run himself into the ground, and he got a standing ovation from his team-mates on the touchline bench when he was substituted in the closing stages as Franz Beckenbauer looked for ways to shore up his tiring defence.

Holland were doing their best to pull themselves back into the game and would have pulled level but for a shocking miskick by van Basten after he had been put clear by Gullit, who was causing the Germans problems with his speed and sharpness despite a heavily strapped right thigh. Just as the Dutch looked

65

as if they had got their momentum going in time to save the match, the adventurous Brehme, one of the greatest of all attacking full-backs, motored down the left before curling a looping shot out of reach of goalkeeper Hans van Breukelen and into the far corner of the net in the 85th minute.

Holland still refused to give up but were lucky to get a consolation goal in the last minute when what appeared to be a dive by van Basten earned a penalty from which Ronald Koeman scored.

So Holland went out of the World Cup after a gutsy and at times poetic performance following three below-par showings in the group matches. They must wonder what they have to do to beat the Germans in world championship contests. This was their fifth loss in five World Cup duels.

 Saint comments

West Germany deserved to win this explosive encounter against a Dutch side that was too often more interested in settling vendettas than in getting on with the game. Some of the football played by both teams was quite breathtaking, and it is difficult to imagine any team stopping the Germans reaching the final if they can maintain this pace and power.

I was particularly taken with the performance of the veteran Pierre Littbarski, who managed to give Klinsmann good support despite the close attentions of Adrie van Tiggelen. Klinsmann had a great game, and must surely now have won over the German fans who have always been ultra critical of him.

Like Greavsie, I was disgusted with the behaviour of Frank Rijkaard. It followed a lot of bitter and inflammatory things that were said during interviews before the match, but no matter what the provocation there is never any excuse for what Rijkaard did in full view of millions of TV viewers. He is an outstanding player, but has scarred his image for life. He will always be remembered as the man who was sent off in a World Cup match for spitting. The motto for all footballers should be: PLEASE DO NOT SPIT.

Juergen Klinsmann, West Germany's goal hero: "That was the most beautiful game of my life, and I shall treasure for always the memory of my goal. Rudi was very unlucky to be sent off and I made up my mind to play for both of us. We always have very hard matches against Holland, and this one was difficult for both teams because there was so much at stake. I was sorry to be called off because I had been enjoying the game so much, but I have to admit that I had tired myself out. It was hard work without Rudi there at my side. We are very much a team and work for each other."

Franz Beckenbauer, West Germany's manager: "The referee was quite right to send off Rijkaard, but I was very disappointed to see him also dismiss Voeller when he was obviously not the guilty party. Rijkaard spat in his face three times. That sort of behaviour does not belong in football. It is the greatest possible insult and I condemn it most deeply. We thoroughly deserved our victory. There was some disorder in our game at the beginning, but the longer it went on the more we had it under control. This is quite the best German team I have ever been associated with. We have had outstanding sides in the past, but none that can match this team for togetherness and spirit. We are taking each game as it comes and are not interested at this stage in talking about the possibility of winning the World Cup."

Jack Charlton, Ireland's outspoken manager, when interviewed by Greavsie on his reaction to the sending off of Frank Rijkaard for spitting: "I'll tell you what I would have done if he had spat at me when I was playing – I would have chinned him."

Facing page: Rudi Voeller and Frank Rijkaard get their marching orders after a flare-up that shamed World Cup '90

Monday June 25   Phase 2
Rep. of Ireland (0) **0**, **Romania** (0) **0**
Genoa   *Ireland won 5-4 on penalties*

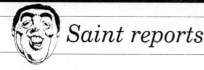 *Saint reports*

In a heart-stopping finale Ireland staggered into the World Cup quarter-finals with a penalties victory over Romania after the two teams had finished deadlocked following extra time. This tournament is becoming like something out of the imagination of a Hollywood scriptwriter, and this latest contribution from Jack Charlton's boyos stretched the belief factor to the limit.

There was an entire team of Irish heroes, but none stood taller or was more widely toasted in Dublin's taverns than goalkeeper Pat Bonner and Arsenal veteran David O'Leary. With the score in the penalty shoot-out standing at four successful spot-kicks each, Celtic goalie Bonner flung himself to his right to push away Daniel Timofte's penalty. Danny boy was close to tears as Bonner – Packy to all his pals – leapt in joyful celebration.

Then striding on to the centre stage came David O'Leary with enough responsibility on his shoulders to sink a battleship. He has been an outstanding servant for Ireland, but it is no secret that he and big Jack Charlton have never really hit it off. He has yet to be selected to start a World Cup match, and found himself summoned into this one only as a substitute in the first half of extra time.

I cannot recall ever seeing David take a penalty before, but there could not have been a steadier hand on the trigger as he placed the ball and looked long and hard in the direction of goalkeeper Silviu Lung like a gunfighter weighing up the opposition before going for his weapon. Then he took three paces back, stopped for one more range-finding look and finally stepped forward and fired a rising shot to the right of Lung, who dived the wrong way and was on his knees like a beaten boxer as the ball flashed into the back of the net for what rivalled Niall Quinn's effort against Holland as

the greatest goal in the history of Irish football. It was certainly the most important.

I was thrilled and privileged to be there in the Genoa stadium to share the joy of this momentus achievement by the Irish footballers in general and Jack Charlton in particular. Jack and I go back a long way, and I have always admired his straight forward approach to the job of management. There is no side to the man whatsoever and he says exactly what he thinks regardless of whether or not it will make him popular. We used to be in harness at Sheffield Wednesday when I was his coach, and he has carried his ideas of direct, no-nonsense play of those days into the international arena. Along the way he has also become a master of blarney, and he has kidded the world about his team. He has allowed everybody to fall into the trap of thinking they are just a bunch of kick-and-rush tearaways, while in actual fact there is an enormous amount of skill running right the way through the side.

If you want facts to support my feeling that Ireland are a much more efficient team than people have been led to believe, just let me point out that this was their 17th successive match without defeat and in those games they have conceded just four goals. Jack Charlton and his sidekick Maurice Setters have been in charge for 42 games, and in 27 Ireland have not allowed the opposition to put the ball into their net. That's some record, and it will be causing concern in the Italian camp as they prepare for the quarter-final showdown with Ireland in Rome.

The secret of Ireland's success is the way all of the players work for each other. Jack has fired them up with a team spirit that rages like a furnace. You only have to look at the midfield maurauding of Mick McGrath, Ray Houghton, Andy Townsend and Kevin Sheedy to realise why they are so hard to beat and so difficult to play against. They cover marathon distances – often at sprint speed – and any opponent who dwells on the ball finds himself the victim of an ambush by green-shirted players.

On paper, Romania looked to have a decided edge in skill and penetrative powers. But on the pitch this was cancelled out by Ireland's work rate. In Gheorghe Hagi Romania had one of the most gifted players in the entire tourna-

ment, yet even he after a promising start stuttered rather than strutted as the Irish closed him down every time he tried to open the way to goal. It was unfortunate for Romania that their main striker Marius Lacatus was suspended, but let nothing detract from a magnificent Irish performance.

For the record, Sheedy, Houghton, Townsend and Tony Cascarino all safely converted their penalties before O'Leary's date with destiny. And I cannot possibly finish this report without a merit mention for the Irish fans. They filled the stadium with happy noise, and there was not a spot of bother from them. Along with the Scots, they put the hooligan element among England's following to shame.

Greavsie comments

I honestly believe that Ireland are one of the few teams left in the finals who just might prove a handful for Italy. Jack O'Charlton has got them playing out of their skins, and their drive, their determination and their sheer exuberance will cancel out much of the skill advantages held by the Italians. You had to have sympathy with Romania going out to the cruel penalties system. Surely it would be fairer to decide the winners on the number of corners forced. As a matter of interest, Ireland would also have won on this score.

Pat Bonner dives to glory as he makes the vital penalty save that set up Ireland for victory

QUOTE UNQUOTE

Jack Charlton, Ireland's manager: "This is even more special for me than when I was in England's 1966 World Cup-winning team. I promised people we were going to Rome, and now we can't wait to get there to take on Italy. I'll tell you this – don't bet against us. I would not have fancied the pressure David O'Leary had on him, but he took his penalty like the real pro he is. We've had a few words to say to each other, but everything's fine between us. We're all pulling together for the team. We haven't won or lost a game here yet. We'll be happy to win the Cup in a penalty shoot-out!"

David O'Leary, the penalty hero: "I couldn't let Packy Bonner down after that great save of his. He had been on the wrong end of a defeat in a penalty shoot-out after the Scottish Cup Final a few weeks back. I made up my mind where I was going to shoot the ball before I placed it on the spot. It was my first ever goal for Ireland and my proudest moment in football."

Monday June 25   Phase 2
Italy (0) **2**, **Uruguay** (0) **0**
Rome

 Greavsie reports

Salvatore Schillaci, the hit-man from Sicily, has done it again. Just as Italy were beginning to run out of ideas about how to break down Uruguay's stubborn defence he unleashed the shot of the tournament to knock the World Cup life out of the South Americans.

In football-daft Italy Schillaci now comes second in popularity only to the Pope since his emergence as the man who can be relied on to stick the ball into the net.

Their team was like a sleek Ferrari without oomph until he came roaring off the substitutes' bench in the first match against Austria, and he has since grown in stature and strength with every appearance. He very nearly

Salvatore Schillaci, the Sicilian hitman, fires in the shot that gives Italy the lead against Uruguay

scored the quickest World Cup goal of all time after just 20 seconds but screwed a shot on the turn wide of the target. Italy got the ball into the Uruguayan net midway through the first half when £8 million striker Roberto Baggio struck a fierce free kick wide of the defensive wall. Goalkeeper Fernando Alvez had the discipline and sense not to make a move for the ball because he saw English referee George Courtney signalling that it was an indirect free kick.

Italy looked in danger of conceding their first goal of the tournament when a rare defensive error by Fernando de Napoli allowed Carlos Aguilera a sight of goal. He rifled in a rising shot that gave Walter Zenga the chance to show why he is rated the greatest Italian goalkeeper since Dino Zoff, and as he plucked the ball out of the air we realised how it is that he has not let a goal past him for ten successive international matches.

There was so much at stake in this match

70

that both teams were almost choking with the tension, and referee Courtney had to be firm to stop volatile temperaments getting out of control.

Alvez made a wonder save 15 minutes into the second half when he threw himself across goal to fingertip a curling free kick from Luigi de Agostini around a post, and this inspired the Uruguayans to concentrate even harder on their disciplined and determined defensive system that was slowly throttling the life out of the Italians. The prospect of Italy being taken into extra time was just beginning to enter our heads when Schillaci exploded into action in the 66th minute. Zenga's long kick delivered the ball to the feet of Baggio, who transferred it to Aldo Serena. There seemed nothing on as he sent the ball diagonally through to Schillaci, who was closely marked and apparently left with little room in which to manoeuvre. But in the blinking of an eye he had the ball in the back of the net with an incredible dipping, instant left-foot shot from just outside the penalty area.

It was a blinder of a goal, and it lifted the pressure off Italy and gave them the confidence to unfurl the full range of their attacking skills. Uruguay were now rushed off their feet and they conceded a second goal in the 83rd minute when Serena headed in a measured free kick from the multi-talented Giuseppe Giannini. Italy were looking more and more the part of eventual finalists.

 ## Saint comments

There was something almost inevitable about this Italian win. Well as Uruguay played there was rarely a moment when you could envisage them piercing an Italian defence in which sweeper Franco Baresi stands out like a lighthouse surrounded by rocks. I honestly think that the only type of side that might unsettle the smoothest Italian team I have ever seen is one playing fast and direct stuff – a style perfected by Jack Charlton's Ireland. Their quarter-final in Rome is going to be a fascinating duel, and as Jack keeps telling me every time I see him in Italy – "don't bet against us".

Giuseppe Bergomi, Italy's captain: "Uruguay made it very difficult for us, and it was not until Salvatore's magnificent goal that we were able to start to relax and play the sort of football that we know our public enjoys. All our thoughts are now centred on the quarter-final match against Ireland. I played against the Republic in Dublin five years ago, and we had to work hard for a 2–1 victory. We will need to be as physically strong as them, and then I believe our extra pace in attack will show to great advantage. Their record proves that they are an excellent team, but we have the weapons to beat them."

Salvatore Schillaci, scorer of Italy's first goal: "That was as beautiful a goal as I have ever scored, but I must give credit to Serena. He gave me a perfect pass. It is still hard to believe that this is all happening to me. I was the last player selected for the squad, and I am sure most people thought I would spend the finals sitting on the touchline bench. My job is to score goals, and I hope I have more to come before the tournament is over."

Azeglio Vicini, Italy's manager: "Schillaci has achieved more for us than we ever dared hope. Irrespective of his goals he has played exceptionally well, and has helped ease what was a worrying injury problem. Gianluca Vialli and Roberto Donadoni are both about to resume full training and will come into the reckoning for team selection for the quarter-final match against Ireland. It may be a blessing in disguise that they have missed games because they are now fresh. Some of our players are tired, and there are all sorts of permutations I shall be considering for the quarter-final. We know Ireland are very strong in the air and we shall be looking to counter this. People keep talking about us being the favourites, but we are simply concentrating on one game at a time. There is a long way still to go."

Tuesday June 26   Phase 2
Spain (0) **1, Yugoslavia** (0) **2**
Verona *(after extra time; 1–1 at 90 mins)*

 Saint reports

It was the genius of Dragan Stojkovic that finally separated these two evenly matched teams as he revealed to the world why Marseilles have recently agreed to invest £5 million to import his talent to France. Stojkovic struck two goals for Yugoslavia that will be contenders when the "greatest goals of World Cup '90" are considered.

The game was played in fierce heat that seemed to drain most of the players of real ambition, and they played at a pace that suggested from an early stage that minds were tuned to conserving energy for the possibility of extra time.

Spain created enough chances to have clinched a place in the quarter-finals for the first time since 1950, but they squandered their opportunities. Their biggest culprit was Emilio Butragueño, an idolised player with Real Madrid who is nicknamed "The Vulture". He got the bird from his own supporters as he twice missed sitters in front of goal. Spanish manager Luis Suarez was preparing to substitute the out-of-touch Butragueño at the very moment that Stojkovic gave a lesson in how to finish in the 77th minute.

Zlatko Vujovic made a run deep into Spanish territory despite crude attempts by Manuel Sanchis to halt his progress. He crossed the ball to the near post where Srecko Katanec headed it on to the centre of the goalmouth. Stojkovic brought the ball under control as calmly as if he was in a training session, sent his marker skidding into empty space with a dip of his shoulder and then slipped the ball past goalkeeper Andoni Zubizarreta. He passed rather than shot the ball into the net in a stunning style reminiscent of how a certain wee man called Greavsie used to do it. There can be no higher praise.

Spain's World Cup life seemed to be ebbing

Dragan Stojkovic, scorer of two classic goals for Yugoslavia against Spain

away until Julio Salinas got on the end of a deflected cross from Martin Vazquez and prodded the ball into the net at the far post.

The game was just two minutes into extra time when Stojkovic conjured a Brazilian-style free kick from 20 yards, bending it around the defensive wall and into the net out of reach of Zubizarreta's despairing dive.

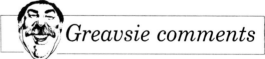 *Greavsie comments*

There will not be a more talented player in the quarter-finals than Dragan Stojkovic. He was the player who prompted me to select Yugoslavia as outsiders for the World Cup, and if a few more of his team-mates were on the same wave-length then there would be no holding the Yugoslavs. The battle for supremacy between Stojkovic and Maradona in the quarter-final could be one of the great duels of World Cup '90.

Tuesday June 26 Phase 2	
England (0) **1**, **Belgium** (0) **0**	
Bologna *After extra time*	

David Platt volleys in his dramatic winner for England against Belgium in the last minute of extra time. The official time for the goal was given as the 119th minute

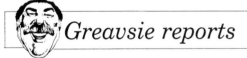

Greavsie reports

David Platt became the latest player to write his name large on a World Cup tournament that could have been produced and directed by Alfred Hitchcock. The Aston Villa captain stepped into this full-blooded thriller as a substitute, and with a penalty shoot-out just seconds away he scored a phenomenal first goal for England to lift them into the quarter-finals.

It has to be conceded that England were slightly fortunate to beat a Belgian team that had the edge in all-round skill, but in football you make your own luck and nobody can argue that Bobby Robson's players did not deserve reward for all their endeavour and their occasional classical movements that suggested they

are coming to the boil at just the right time.

The match was played at a furious pace until the intense heat slowed just about everybody down to an exhausted jog in extra time. Both teams were a credit to football with their sportsmanship, and they gave a lesson to all the play-actors who are causing so much irritation in these finals in how to get up and get on with the game after being tackled.

England got off to a nervous start and might easily have been two or three goals down in the opening 15 minutes following errors by Terry Butcher, Paul Parker and Mark Wright, but the Belgians seemed surprised to find the path to goal opening up so easily and made a mess of their chances. Parker in particular was struggling to get into the game, but after his neurotic opening spell he settled down to become one of the most effective defenders on the pitch.

Enzo Scifo was bossing the game for Bel-

73

74

gium despite the close attentions of the industrious Steve McMahon, and his intelligent running and precise passing were causing consternation in the England defence. The veteran Jan Ceulemans rode an attempted tackle by Mark Wright on the edge of the penalty area and his rising shot smacked high against Peter Shilton's right post.

Wright then very nearly scored a carbon copy of the goal he netted against Holland when he was just inches wide with a glancing header from a Paul Gascoigne free kick. Gazza was being overshadowed in midfield by the silky-smooth Scifo, but I admired his control in the often fierce exchanges and he did enough creatively again to justify Bobby Robson's growing faith in him.

Chris Waddle was putting together his most telling performance of the finals, and at last he was taking on and beating opponents. He was continually exposing the Belgian defenders to the perils of panic as he danced past their challenges, but without being able to create a deadlock-breaking goal.

John Barnes on the other wing was again almost anonymous. He shot feebly after being put clear in front of goal following enterprising overlapping work by Stuart Pearce. But Barnes was desperately unlucky in the 40th minute when he steered in a beautiful cross from Gary Lineker for what looked an excellent goal. A linesman ended England's celebrations as, wrongly in my opinion, he waved the goal off side.

But luck has a habit of balancing out in football, and early in the second half it was Belgium's turn to think the gods were against them when Scifo hammered in a low shot from 30 yards. Peter Shilton was as much a spectator as I as the ball flashed past him and cannoned off his right post for the second time.

It was round about this time that I began to think how much England were missing their injury-cursed skipper Bryan Robson, who had gone home the previous day for an operation on his damaged Achilles tendon. His deputy, McMahon, was doing a noble job in midfield, but I felt Robson would have made his pre-

Facing page: Paul "Gazza" Gascoigne, the fastest tongue in the west, after flooring Enzo Scifo

sence felt in the Belgian penalty area. Had I been in the shoes of manager Bobby Robson I would have pulled off the ineffective Barnes and sent on the fresh David Platt to make attacking runs from a midfield base. I got it half right, but once again Bobby confounded me with his decision. He sent Platt on but in place of McMahon, which meant that dangerman Scifo was suddenly left without a minder.

I considered that Barnes was guilty of unprofessionalism at this point. He was suffering from a recurrence of a groin injury and should have made it known to the touchline bench that he was not 100 per cent fit. Shortly after McMahon had been called off, he signalled to the bench that his injury had worsened and Steve Bull was sent on in his place.

Platt had a chance to score a goal with his very first touch when he got deep into Belgian territory, but he hooked his shot just off target. It was an encouraging sign that he was prepared to have a go.

Former Tottenham winger Nico Claesen came into the Belgian attack from the substitutes' bench, and he threatened to create a goal when he outpaced Des Walker who was struggling with an ankle injury. Much to the relief of England, Claesen failed to find either of two team-mates who were loitering with intent in the middle.

Gascoigne, missing the protective shield that McMahon had provided, made a reckless tackle on the menacing Scifo and became the only player in the match shown the yellow card, which was quite remarkable considering that referees in these finals have been taking names like over-zealous autograph hunters.

Players on both sides were on the edge of exhaustion as the game went into extra time. Pearce was troubled by cramp, Walker was bravely pushing himself through a pain barrier and skipper Butcher was hobbling. The spectators jeered as Gascoigne brought the game down to walking pace, playing keep-ball rather than risk Belgium winning possession. It might have looked negative, but Gazza was wisely protecting his injured team-mates and it looked as if England had settled on trusting their luck to the Russian roulette of a penalty shoot-out.

Then, with one minute of extra time to

go and as we were wondering which players would be put on the spot for England, Gascoigne dug down into his reserves of stamina for one last run from midfield. He was shadowed by veteran Belgian captain Eric Gerets, who had played a storming match but was dragging his tired legs trying to keep up with Gazza. In his desperation he tripped Gascoigne, and the referee blew for a free kick 25 yards from goal. It would have been easy for the tired Gascoigne to have played a simple free kick just so that England could retain possession, but he elected to send one of his floaters deep into the penalty area. Platt watched it carefully like a plane spotter, and spun round to face the goal as the ball dropped over his shoulder. All in the same movement he volleyed it wide of goalkeeper Michel Preud'-Homme. It would have been rated a classic goal in any football match. In the last minute of a World Cup finals tie it must go down as one of the greatest goals ever scored for England.

 *Saint comments*

Fortune favoured the brave in Bologna where England carved out a victory that owed as much to their willpower as to their skill. Make no mistake, Belgium were one of the more talented teams in this tournament, but England had the better of them when it came to honest endeavour. Once again England played the sweeper system with great success, and without the spare man at the back I doubt if they would have been able to master a Belgian team for whom Scifo, Ceulemans and Gerets were world-class performers.

It must have been reassuring for Bobby Robson to see Chris Waddle at last producing the twisting, tormenting runs of which we know he is capable, but John Barnes continues to be an enigma. I just cannot believe I am watching the same player who gave a score of blinding displays for Liverpool last season.

This victory has surely opened the door to the semi-finals for England. It's difficult to envisage them losing to Cameroon. But I harboured the same thoughts before the Africans played Argentina!

David Platt, England's goal hero: "I can hardly believe it's happened. Just two years ago I was playing in the Fourth Division with Crewe. I would have told anybody they were mad if they had said then that I would be scoring a vital goal in the 1990 World Cup finals. The timing of it could not have been better, I suppose. It meant Belgium did not have a chance of getting back into the game. I've no idea whether I shall be playing in the quarter-final against Cameroon. That will be up to the gaffer. We're a squad and we all accept that he can only pick 11 players. We have a terrific spirit running right the way through the squad, and after this victory our confidence is sky high. "

Bobby Robson, England's manager: "We won this one for our skipper Bryan Robson. It was devastating for him to have to miss out yet again because of injury. As he left us to go home for an operation we promised him that we would win this match. This victory has given us a feeling of buoyancy. We're in the last eight, with a great chance of reaching the semis. We will not underestimate Cameroon. Any team that can beat Argentina, Romania and Colombia deserves the utmost respect."

Guy Thys, manager of Belgium: "We consider ourselves very unlucky not to have won. It was heart-breaking to concede a goal so close to the end. The match seemed certain to go to penalties, and then the result would have been in the lap of the gods. It was just not meant that we should win this game. We twice hit the woodwork with goalkeeper Shilton beaten. We have in no way been disgraced, and our players can feel proud of their efforts.The England players who impressed me most were Waddle, who was very clever on the ball, and Gascoigne, who I am sure is going to develop into a very good footballer indeed. I feel sure that they can beat Cameroon but, in football, who dare predict anything?"

World Cup chat-a-thon

We have now reached the quarter-finals, Greavsie, and I think it's a blow for football that Brazil are no longer part of the tournament. And before you make any of your sarcastic comments, I am not saying that because I tipped them to win the World Cup. I just feel they had so much more to offer, and they play the sort of easy-on-the-eye football that gives the ideal lead for the millions of youngsters watching the finals on worldwide television.

I understand what you mean, but at the end of the day they have only themselves to blame for going out. They always looked a superior side to Argentina, but what they lacked was a real diamond of a player who could put the finishing touch to all their artistry. Their great teams of the past always had a handful of world-class forwards. This time around they had plenty of good players, yet not one who could be classed in the great category. Careca looked the part in short bursts, but – like the team – he lacked consistency.

If there was any justice, Brazil would have gone through to the last eight instead of Argentina who have hardly strung together a dozen decent moves in all their matches so far. This was the most disciplined Brazilian team I have ever seen. They were challenging and closing down opponents, and you could see the influence of European football that has been introduced by their squad of players who now play their club football on this side of the Atlantic. In a way I suppose the new defensive discipline has robbed them of some of their flair, and I know that Pelé was particularly outspoken against manager Sebastiao Lazaroni for going against pure Brazilian traditions. Yet surely the balance between football the Brazilian way and football the European way would be the perfect way to play?

Giller

NORMAL SERVICE WILL BE RESUMED WHEN BELGIUM GIVE US THE BALL BACK

Perhaps the time has come for us to stop looking at the Brazilians as the leaders of world football. It is 20 years since they last won the World Cup, and they never really showed anything extra special in these finals to suggest that they could have gone all the way. For me, West Germany and Italy are the only two outstanding teams in the tournament. One of the biggest disappointments was the failure of Holland to function at anything like their full pace and power. Marco van Basten had a nightmare, and I wonder if he will be able to get it out of his system. There were reports coming out of Holland that he is sick to death of the sight of a football. Perhaps a long rest would be the answer for him. He needs to recharge his batteries.

It has to be said, Greavsie, that the gods are smiling on England. I thought Belgium were the better side, and in Enzo Scifo they had one of the best players in the tournament. That effort of his that rocked the England post was one of the

77

great shots of the tournament. I'm not sure Peter Shilton knew the ball had gone past him until he heard it hit the woodwork.

I agree it was a super shot, but it takes second place to Schillaci's rocket against Uruguay. I don't think I have ever seen a ball dip quite as viciously, and I thought it must have got a deflection. Schillaci is becoming *the* sensation of the finals and I wonder how Jack O'Charlton's Ireland are going to counter his menace in the quarter-final. Ireland have performed miracles getting this far, and they will give Italy plenty of trouble with their straight-for-the-jugular style of play, but I believe it is now going to be a case of *arrivederci Roma* for Jack and his boyos.

If any team can beat Italy it's Ireland. They have nothing to lose and all the pressure will be on the Italians. Their fans are now worked up into a frenzy and are convinced the World Cup is theirs for the taking. They would be making the mistake of a lifetime to underestimate Ireland. Like you, I think Italy will win but it's going to be mighty close. Those people who think it will be a walk-over for Italy are going to be in for a shock. The same goes for England in their match against Cameroon. They should win, but it is likely to be tight.

England are fortunate to have been alerted to the dangers posed by Cameroon. They were an unknown quantity at the start of the finals and everybody expected them to be a side of Aunt Sallies. Their victories over Argentina, Romania and Colombia have opened all eyes to their talent, and we know we cannot afford to underestimate them. Roger Milla is a wily striker from the old school, but if he comes on our defence will know exactly what to expect. I cannot see us allowing him the room that he has been given in his previous appearances. The game looks made for a player of Chris Waddle's skill. I think he and Gazza could have a field day against Cameroon, and I will be surprised if we do not win by two clear goals. How's that for confidence?

"A late news item – Diego Maradona has won yet another award. He has been voted Best Actor in Italia '90."

Confidence is all right, provided it does not slide into complacency. So come on, Greavsie, which three teams do you pick for the semi-finals along with England?

I'll take Italy to beat Ireland 1–0, West Germany to bounce the Czechs 3–1 and Argentina to muddle through to a 1–— victory over Yugoslavia, perhaps after extra-time. It could be easier if Maradona stops diving around and gets on with the game. Which are your last four teams?

The same as yours, but I would not be too surprised if Ireland caused a major upset by knocking out Italy. I hope Yugoslavia beat Argentina, because I would like to see Dragan Stojkovic parading his skill in the final. He's one of my favourite players of the tournament, but I don't think he has enough team-mates able to meet and match his standards. The Czechs might give West Germany a few shocks before they go out. I just hope we don't have a repeat of the nastiness that crept into Germany's match against Holland. That spitting incident involving Frank Rijkaard and Rudi Voeller was the worst of all the scars on this tournament.

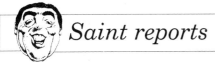
Saint reports

Argentina, wearing their luck for all to see like a magic cloak, clawed their way into the semi-finals after an amazing penalty shoot-out against a Yugoslavian side that must wonder what they have done to upset the footballing gods.

The world champions survived the closest of calls when poor Faruk Hadzibegic missed Yugoslavia's fifth spot-kick which would have levelled the scores at 3–3 and taken the penalty deciders into sudden death. This had all the tension and drama of the Gunfight at the OK Corral, but if the shooting accuracy had been the same in that famous western show-down Wyatt Earp and Doc Holliday would have emptied their guns with few notches to boast about. Diego Maradona and Dragan Stojkovic, two players you would put your house on to score from the penalty spot, were among the five players who missed the target in a sensational climax to an otherwise forgettable match.

Yet again Argentina failed to produce anything like their 1986 world championship form, and for long periods they were outfought and out-thought by Yugoslavia. From the 32nd minute the Yugoslavs had to function with only ten men after Refik Sabanadzovic had been shown the red card for tripping Maradona, whose biggest contribution to the game was to dive to the floor the moment anybody breathed on him. It's no secret that Maradona is carrying an injury, but he is also carrying his dying swan act too far and it's about time he was warned to cut out his theatrical tantrums.

Sabanadzovic had earlier been shown the yellow card for not being 10 yards off the ball at a free kick. It was just the latest farce in the procession of joke decisions by referees who have been turned into card-pulling clowns by

A distraught Dragan Stojkovic takes cover after his miss from the penalty spot in the shoot-out against Argentina.

FIFA's disciplinary directive that appears to have left no room for discretion.

The Yugoslavs shrugged off the handicap of being a man short and continued to dominate the game with beautifully constructed movements that usually had their birth at the artistic feet of Stojkovic, who has continually splashed bright colours on the World Cup canvas. He teased and tormented the Argentinian defenders with neat, accurate passes that gave you the impression he could have threaded the ball through the eye of a needle.

Yugoslavia had another outstanding performer in 21-year-old Robert Prosinecki, whose shock of blond hair gave him a Scandinavian appearance while his football seemed more of the Brazilian variety. He patrolled imaginatively in midfield as if he, rather than Maradona, was the superstar, and his power-propelled runs and bold passes earmarked him as a player to note for the future.

Yet for all their territorial advantage against the lethargic world champions, Yugoslavia were unable to convert their superiority into the currency of goals. In fact they were squandering their chances like repentant misers, and slowly they ran out of belief in themselves and started to play as negatively as Argentina. The best chances of the match fell to Dejan Savicevic, who came cold into the game as a substitute in the 62nd minute. He was still settling to the pedestrian pace of the match when first Stojkovic and then Prosinecki put him clear with only goalkeeper Sergio Goycochea to beat. Each time he snatched at his shot and let Argentina off the hook.

The Argentinians, with Maradona never getting out of third gear, relied heavily on the thrust of Jorge Burruchaga in their rare counter-attacks, but he lacked his usual finishing power and precision after getting himself into promising positions deep in the Yugoslavian penalty area.

The sterile game staggered into extra time, with the players clearly affected by fierce temperatures of around 30°C. Just as everything was pointing to a penalty shoot-out, Burruchaga bundled the ball into the Yugoslavian net two minutes from the end of extra time. But before Argentinian celebrations could get under way, Swiss referee Kurt Rothlisberger over ruled the goal because he had spotted Burruchaga helping the ball on its way with an arm. This prompted Maradona to stir himself into his first totally committed activity of the afternoon. The man whose "Hand of God" had helped eliminate England in the 1986 quarter-finals charged in a fury after the referee and then continued his protests for several minutes on the touchline, with FIFA officials rightly insisting that the referee's decision was final. The sight of Maradona complaining so vehemently over a goal being disallowed for hand-ball must have caused amusement and ironic cheers the length and breadth of England.

Action replays proved the referee right, and it would have been a travesty of justice if Yugoslavia had been beaten by another illegal goal by Argentina.

But the Yugoslavian misery had merely been delayed. The penalty shoot-out started with Jose Serrizuela planting the ball into the back of the net for Argentina. Then Stojkovic, of all people, smacked the ball against the top of the bar. Argentinia 1, Yugoslavia 0. Burruchaga and Prosinecki safely converted their penalties. Argentina 2, Yugoslavia 1. Then it was the turn of the Argentinians to be put on the rack when first Maradona and then Pedro Troglio failed to find the back of the net, and Savicevic levelled it at 2–2. The roar from the crowd when Maradona made a mess of his spot-kick could have been heard right across Florence. The wee man is loved in his adopted home town of Naples, but is clearly loathed in every other corner of Italy.

Gustavo Dezotti steered in Argentina's fifth penalty to give them a 3–2 advantage. So it all hung on Hadzibegic, who looked a bag of nerves as he walked into the penalty area to place the ball. He took aim but then shot tamely and Goycochea made a comfortable save to put Argentina into the semi-finals.

The Argentines celebrated as if they had just won the World Cup, none more so than Maradona who had yet again come back from the dead. We have seen little of his genius in these finals so far, but such will have been his relief at being let off the hook that he might well be inspired to turn it on against Italy or the Republic of Ireland in the semi-final. This World Cup desperately needs a sparkling individual performance from somebody like Maradona, otherwise it is going to be remembered as the tournament on which few world-class players stamped their personality. In fairness, they have not been helped by a lot of fussy and often infuriating refereeing that robs the games of fluency and rhythm.

Greavsie and I have deliberately not listed many of the record number of bookings in these finals because so many of them have been for the pettiest of so-called offences. At times the players have been treated as if they were in a kindergarten, and the slightest hint of physical contact has had the quick-on-the-draw referees reaching for their yellow cards like demented members of the Magic Circle.

I mention it here because it is worth noting that three Argentinian players received yellow cards in this match – Serrizuela, Olarti-coechea and Simon, and each of them was booked for cynical fouls against the most accomplished player on view, Stojkovic. It brings the total of Argentinian players cautioned to date to 11, all of whom are now walking a tightrope in the semi-final.

They include goalkeeper Goycochea and their temperamental captain Maradona. A booking for any one of them in the semi-final and they would automatically be banned from the final, that is of course if they make it to Rome on July 8. And the way they are riding their luck, don't count them out just yet.

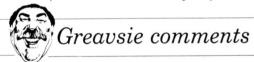 *Greavsie comments*

With Argentina's luck they could nick the World Cup while playing the least effective football in their history. I know England were fortunate against Belgium, but at least they earned their luck with their honest endeavour.

There was little honest effort from the Argentinians, who rolled around as if shot after every tackle. The standard of refereeing has slumped from the acceptable to the appalling, and Maradona and his men played this referee like a violin. They even tried to cheat their way to a goal, as in 1986, and it was tragic to see a vastly superior Yugoslav side go out in such a cruel manner. While the penalty shoot-outs give spectators excitement, they are an unfair burden on exhausted players and I repeat that it would be fairer to judge a dead-locked match on the number of corners that have been forced by the end of extra time. This would encourage attacking play, rather than the negative approach we are seeing as teams play it safe so that they can gamble on the Russian roulette of penalties.

Carlos Bilardo, Argentina's manager who is giving up the job after World Cup '90 because he considers the pressures too great: "My heart stopped when Maradona missed his penalty. Perhaps we are asking too much of him. I don't know how he manages to get out on to the pitch for each match with his ankle injury. But he insists on playing for his country. It is going to be a race for us to get him fit for the semi-final. His ankle is swollen and very, very sore. I reject the suggestions that we are lucky. We all know that in football you make your own luck. We are battling through with injured players, and we are unable to train properly and make the right preparations for each match. It is very difficult to get any sort of momentum going, but we will be aiming to raise our game for the semi-final."

Ivica Osim, Yugoslavia's coach who refused to talk to reporters from his own country after they had printed stories that he had drunk six bottles of whisky in celebration of their group win over Colombia: "My players did not deserve this. They were tired after all the effort they had put in, and when you are tired you lose your concentration. This is why we missed the penalties. But anybody who saw the match would have to admit that the best team lost."

Diego Maradona, Argentina's controversial captain: "I look forward to playing in the semi-final at Naples. It is my favourite ground in all the world, and the fans there are my fans. We have a thing between us. I love playing for them and they love watching me play. Even if we meet Italy I believe many of them will be on my side. I have been very saddened by the behaviour of many of the spectators. They have not shown the usual respect to the playing of national anthems, and I have had to get used to a lot of shrieking every time I touch the ball. But I will not get this treatment in Naples. That is where I always feel at home."

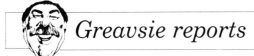

Greavsie reports

Irish eyes were still smiling after their World Cup adventure ended with a narrow defeat by a magnificent Italian team that was scared down to its socks by Jack O'Charlton's battling boyos. There was no need for an Irish wake, because at this World Cup we had been in on the birth rather than the death of Ireland as a formidable force in football.

Big Jack has had to face savage criticism of his team's tactics and methods but, like their positive style or not, nobody can deny that he has managed to turn a backwoods football country into a power to be reckoned with and respected on the international stage.

As with every team they have faced over the past three or so years, Ireland imposed themselves on Italy – or, as my old England team-mate Jack puts it, "we *inflict* ourselves on the opposition". The impressive result was that for the first time in these finals we saw even the great Franco Baresi, the outstanding defender in the tournament, look rattled as football the Irish way rained in on him.

Ireland came closer than any team in the tournament to getting the ball past Italian goalkeeper Walter Zenga. Paul McGrath had him stretching across his goal to save a header as the Irish piled on the pressure in the early stages. The driving power was coming from midfield where Ray Houghton, McGrath, Andy Townsend and Kevin Sheedy were swarming after the ball and the smooth-as-butter Italian schemers were getting trampled on in the stampede.

At the peak of their effort Ireland very nearly snatched a goal that had been planned and plotted on the playing fields of Dublin.

Facing page: They came, they saw and they so nearly conquered. Jack Charlton reacts to defeat at the end of the match against Italy

McGrath, who has had a tremendous tournament as a versatile anchorman and auxiliary attacker, delivered a superbly directed cross from the right in the 26th minute. Niall Quinn, 6ft 4in of towering inferno, climbed above the Italian defence to ram in a header that brought an acrobatic save from Zenga.

Then, with a hint of what was to come, Salvatore Schillaci – the golden discovery of World Cup '90 – steered Luigi de Agostini's cross only just wide of a post. The Sicilian goal bandit was just warming up. Six minutes before half-time he was involved in the architecture and then the execution of a superb goal. The ball was sent on a pinging path through the Irish defence along a conveyor belt of quick passes involving Giuseppe Giannini, Roberto Baggio, Schillaci and then Giannini again before he placed it on a plate for Roberto Donadoni. His shot from 18 yards was so fierce that goalkeeper Pat Bonner could only block it. The ball ran loose, and while everybody stood and stared Schillaci moved on to it with the enthusiasm of a starving man being invited to a banquet. He drilled the ball low into the net just inside the right-hand post.

For Schillaci, virtually unknown outside Italy before the finals, it was the fourth goal of the tournament. He has scored two with his head, one with his left foot and now another with his right foot. Schillaci is nicknamed "Toto", after an Italian clown. He was now top of the bill at the world football circus.

At this point Ireland were desperately unlucky to be trailing, but with the goal to relax them the Italians started to turn on the tap and out flowed the football that has made them favourites for the title. Seven minutes into the second half Schillaci dug into his treasure chest and came up with another gem of a shot. Giannini guided a caress of a free kick into his path and Toto the clown became Toto the assassin as he unleashed a thunderbolt of a shot. Goalkeeper Bonner was beaten all ends up by the sheer pace of the ball that struck the underside of the bar and rebounded to safety.

Ireland now had to play out of their skins to stay in the game, and against a referee who hardly gave them an inch with his home-favouring decisions. But after Charlton had sent on a new strike force in the shape of first

Tony Cascarino and then John Sheridan, Italy closed up shop. Play-maker Giannini was replaced by the defiant midfield defender Carlo Ancelotti. After a Schillaci goal had been ruled off side, Aldo Serena was sent on in place of Baggio, and you realised the depth of talent at the disposal of Italian manager Azeglio Vicini as you looked along a touchline bench that included players of the calibre of Gianluca Vialli and Andrea Carnevale.

Serena had a great chance to tie up the match when he was put clean through by a superb ball from the immaculate Baresi, but he was robbed by a brave save from Bonner who managed to block the ball with his legs.

Ireland were still making Italian nerves jangle, and Cascarino very nearly forced an equaliser and extra time when he got his head to a ball, and Baresi had to move swiftly to nod it off target before berating his team-mates. Italy seem not only determined to win the World Cup, but to do it with the first clean sheet in World Cup history.

 *Saint comments*

Italy are unlikely to get a fiercer challenge in World Cup '90, even if they reach the final (as I'm sure they will). Ireland did themselves proud with their performance, and I just wonder what the outcome might have been if Quinn's powerful header had not been saved by Zenga mid-way through the first-half. Ireland lost the match but won the respect and admiration of the watching world for their tremendous impact on this tournament. They have not won everybody over with their physical style of football, but even the knockers have to concede that Jack Charlton has worked wonders in getting them playing to their strengths.

The more I see Italy the more I admire them. They are so rich in talent that manager Vicini can adjust tactics to suit any situation simply by sending on gifted substitutes to do a given job. I feel as certain as I can be that Italy will carry too much ammunition for Argentina in the semi-final, but there have been so many twists in this World Cup that just about anything can happen.

Jack Charlton, Ireland's manager: "You will never find me happy in defeat, but I have to pay credit to my lads and say they gave everything they had. We frightened the life out of Italy, and that takes some doing because they are one heck of a team. Irish football is now on the world football map. We've earned respect out here, and perhaps people will start to realise there is method in the way we play. We have shown that there is more than one way to play football, and maybe other countries will be inspired to follow our lead. I'd like to pay tribute to the Irish fans. They were just incredible. Now all I want to do is get home, find a quiet stretch of water and do some fishing."

Andy Townsend, Ireland's midfield player: "We were upset at some of the referee's decisions, but we knew what to expect and just got on with the game. It's been a privilege to play in the World Cup, and we feel proud to have reached the last eight. Italy are a marvellous team, but we gave them plenty to think about."

Azeglio Vicini, Italy's manager: "Ireland were as difficult as I expected, and we knew that only a peak performance would do against them. They can feel extremely proud of their efforts in this World Cup. We now must put all our thoughts on the semi-final against Argentina in Naples. That is, of course, Maradona's home ground. I think that the Neapolitans consider themselves first and foremost Italian and they will temporarily forget their support for Maradona and will get behind us. After all, this is a World Cup game, not a club match. They have always supported us well in the past when we have played there."

Salvatore Schillaci, Italy's goal hero: "I must not get too carried away with what is happening. Our main job has still to be done. We want to *win* the World Cup, so I need to try to score more goals."

Saint reports

The scoreline does not tell the story of what was another masterly performance by West Germany. They would not have been flattered by a flattening 4–0 victory over a Czechoslovakian side that revealed none of the attacking flair that had made them one of the more attractive teams in the tournament.

Germany marched into the ninth World Cup semi-final in their history with as efficient a display of football as you could wish to see, and they gave the distinct impression that, if necessary, they could easily have moved up another gear.

The battered Czechs made four goal-line clearances, and goalkeeper Jan Stejskal came to the rescue with several blinding saves after the Germans had torn through the Czech defence with a power that was awesome. Allied to their superior skills was a will to win that was glaringly absent from a Czechoslovakian team that seemed almost resigned to defeat from the first kick. To watch them play you would never have thought the prize for victory was a place in the World Cup semi-finals.

They were clumsy and sometimes crude in defence, and in the 24th minute they became downright careless. They needlessly conceded a penalty after Juergen Klinsmann had forced his way through half-hearted challenges by Frantisek Straka and Jozef Chovanec before they sandwiched him and brought him down in an untidy tangle.

We have seen so many penalty misses in this tournament that a spot-kick suddenly seems a 50–50 affair, rather than the usual gold-plated goal chance. But Lothar Matthaeus had no doubts about where he was going to place the ball. He managed to convince Stejskal that he was going to fire it to his right and then thundered it to his left in a perfect demonstration of how to take a penalty.

The biggest disappointment for me was the virtual non-appearance of Czechoslovakia's long-haired striking partners Tomas Skuhravy and Ivo Knoflicek. I thought they might have asked some searching questions of the German defence, but they hardly raised a gallop between them.

If there is a weakness in this German team it seems to be at the heart of the defence where the big central defenders lack mobility when put under pressure, but they were able to canter through this match without any sort of real examination.

The German attacking movements all sprang from midfield, where the commander-in-chief Matthaeus got energetic support from Guido Buchwald and the veteran Pierre Littbarski, who rolled back the years to produce a vintage performance. Buchwald had two efforts scrambled off the line in the space of a few seconds in the first half, and twice went within inches of scoring in a one-sided second half. Klinsmann, Matthaeus and then the lively Littbarski also had shots saved more by luck than judgement by Czech defenders reduced to a blind panic.

Yet for all their supremacy Germany could not feel they were safely into the semi-final until the final whistle. Helmut Kohl (the Austrian referee *not* the West German chancellor I hasten to add) kept himself busy with fussy decisions that irritated the Czechs. In the 69th minute Lubomir Moravcik, who had been booked for a petty foul in the first half, got himself sent off for arguing for a penalty after he had been tackled by Littbarski. They got tangled up and Moravcik's boot came loose. As he protested he kicked his boot high in the air. The referee interpreted this as dissent and ordered him off. It was just the latest in the long procession of strange decisions that have marred these finals.

Herr Kohl was yet another referee who looked as if he had prepared for this tournament at the Paul Daniels school of magic. He produced six yellow cards, and infuriated the Czechs with what were inconsistent decisions that were usually in the favour of the Germans.

Moravcik became the 12th player sent off , which gives the false impression that this has been a violent tournament. I have witnessed a lot of clumsy and ill-timed tackles, but few that I would put in the category of vicious. The players have not helped by their tiresome diving and rolling to make tackles look much worse than they are. FIFA must act to stamp out this play-acting, but they must also in future give referees more licence to allow bodily contact. Football remains a man's game, and if you take the physical contact away we might as well switch to marbles.

The Germans will have Rudi Voeller back for the semi-final alongside Klinsmann, who has been a revelation since taking on the role of main striker in Voeller's absence. Together they could prove an unstoppable force.

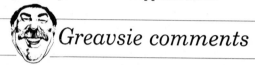 *Greavsie comments*

The Czechs threw in the towel almost from the first kick, and gave West Germany the easiest possible route into the semi-finals. All I can think is that the Czechs have a huge complex about playing Germany, something to do with the history of the two countries. This was not the same Czechoslovakian team that played its earlier matches with a great freedom of spirit and with fast, flowing football.

They were justifiably upset by some refereeing decisions that in my opinion seemed to favour the Germans, but regardless of that the Czechoslovaks were just not in the same class. West Germany go into the semi-finals as top scorers in the tournament with 12 goals. The wonder is that they did not have at least three more under their belt from this match.

We now wait to see whom Germany play in the semi-finals. If, as I hope and believe, it is going to be England they can expect to have a much tougher challenge than came their way from the Czechs. As the Saint says, there is a definite question mark over the middle of the German defence and the team that is bold enough to go at them and exploit the weakness could be rewarded with a place in the World Cup final. But at the moment my money is still on Kaiser Franz's team to make it to the Olympic Stadium in Rome on July 8 for the final.

QUOTE UNQUOTE

Lothar Matthaeus, West Germany's skipper: "I can understand why so many penalties have been missed in these finals. The tension is intolerable as you place the ball, and the target suddenly shrinks. But I was determined not to lose my concentration and made up my mind exactly where I was going to aim the ball. It is a great responsibility, and the relief when you see the ball hit the back of the net is enormous."

Franz Beckenbauer, West Germany's manager: "We have now reached what was our minimum target of a place in the semi-finals. I have made no secret of the fact that I expect a lot from this team. They are exceptional both in style and in spirit. I cannot speak too highly of our captain Lothar Matthaeus. He has been consistently outstanding, and he must surely be in the running for the title of player of the tournament. It is going to be fascinating to see who we meet in the semi-final. I think I would prefer it to be England to Cameroon. We have a great respect for England, but at least we know how they play. Cameroon have been full of surprises."

Jozef Venglos, Czechoslovakia's manager: "West Germany deserved their victory, but we feel the referee was far too harsh on us. His decisions meant that we could not get any momentum going, and we were unable to find the rhythm of our earlier matches. We are not complaining about Germany's penalty, but we were certain that there was one obvious occasion when we might have been awarded one as well. Our team has been excellent, and we wanted to show just how well we could play in this quarter-final. But it was spoiled for us."

Facing page: Master of all he surveys. Lothar Matthaeus, West Germany's captain and chief architect, looks for an opening against Czechoslovakia

Sunday July 1   Quarter-final
Cameroon (0) **2**, **England** (1) **3**
Naples   *After extra time*

Greavsie reports

Gary Lineker scored two goals from the penalty spot not only to put England into the World Cup semi-finals but also to rescue them from one of the most humiliating defeats in their history. The harsh truth is that for long periods Cameroon played England off the park in a dramatic duel that was draining both physically and emotionally, and only a mixture of enormous luck and true grit pulled England through.

More than any other team in the tournament, Cameroon have made World Cup '90 unforgettable. From day one they have injected the elements of surprise and delight into the finals, and if there had been any justice it is they rather than England who would have gone through to a semi-final showdown with West Germany.

Having made my admiration for Cameroon clear I want to balance it with praise for the tremendous character displayed by an England team that reached down into untapped reserves of courage. They hung in and battled away when completely outgunned by a side playing flowing, improvised football that reminded me of the brilliant Brazilians of 1958 when the legend of Pelé was first born.

Pelé was 17 when he exploded on to the World Cup stage. It was a man at the opposite end of his career, 38-year-old Roger Milla, who wrote himself into World Cup folklore against England. The silken skills of substitute Milla were released into the match at the start of the second half with Cameroon unlucky to be trailing 1–0 to an excellent goal that had been burgled by David Platt.

Cameroon had been threatening to take control of the match when Platt struck in the 25th minute. Stuart Pearce made the sort of surging run down the left wing that we had been hoping and expecting to see from John

Gary Lineker switches shirts after his two penalty shots had sunk Cameroon

Barnes and Chris Waddle. Platt, filling the gap left by the sad absence of Bryan Robson, got himself clear in the goalmouth and headed Pearce's precise cross down and into the net from six yards. You could almost feel the relief flooding through the England players because it had been looking as if they were going to be paralysed by a team playing off-the-cuff football that was stunning in its simplicity and explosive in its execution.

Quick, first-time passes and incisive running off the ball continually ripped the England defence apart, and Peter Shilton was called on to show why, even at the age of 40, he is considered one of the world's finest goalkeepers. While Cameroon were sending Milla into urgent action for his fifth appearance in the finals as a substitute, England were pulling off John Barnes, who had again failed to make any sort of impact and was clearly handicapped by a groin injury. Bobby Robson elected to send on Peter Beardsley in his place, but I personally would have given the nod to Steve Bull, whose direct running might have given the Cameroon defence some headaches.

That's the way to do it. Gary Lineker carefully guides home the first of his two penalties against Cameroon

England's new sweeper system was looking decidedly shaky as Milla and the fleet-footed Omam Biyick "one-twoed" the defence into disarray and disorder with rapid exchanges of passes. Paul Gascoigne was back trying to staunch the wounds in the heart of the defence when he collided with Milla and conceded a penalty in the 61st minute. Shilton made a valiant effort to save Emmanuel Kunde's spot-kick with a prodigious dive, but the ball flashed into the net inches away from his outstretched fingertips.

It was during this period that England looked like coming apart at the seams, and in fairness to them I don't think any team in the world could have stood up to the avalanche of attacks being unleashed by the Africans. We had expected them to be weakened by having four players suspended, but they were managing to play better than at any other time in the World Cup. I was particularly taken by the midfield skills of Cyrille Makanaky, who was pulling the strings for the Cameroon attack. Steve McMahon, relegated to the substitutes' bench, must have wondered why he had not

been ordered on to try to subdue him.

Four minutes after earning the penalty for their equaliser the cunning Milla drew defenders towards him before threading a pass through to substitute Eugene Ekeke. He sprinted clear, and then almost casually flicked the ball into the net past Shilton.

It took tremendous nerve and character for England to stay as composed as possible and try to save the match. Bobby Robson sent on Trevor Steven for Terry Butcher. It was a shrewd move because it was pointless continuing with the sweeper system. Steven immediately brought stability to the midfield and it allowed Gascoigne more freedom to start trying to match Cameroon with beautifully improvised skills of his own.

We were starting the countdown on England's World Cup life when, with six minutes to go, Gary Lineker – suddenly sharper and nippier in England's moment of crisis – spun in the penalty area and was brought down by Thomas Libiih. Lineker picked himself up, dusted himself down and scored from the spot to breathe life back into England. If Cameroon were the "Indomitable Lions", then they now knew they were up against British bulldogs.

There was a fresh crisis for England when Mark Wright was cut and badly dazed as he headed the back of Milla's head. He was treated for a jagged gash on his forehead, and then bravely played on through extra time with a huge plaster protecting a wound that later needed seven stitches. It had become a real blood-and-guts battle by England, and they somehow managed to produce their best football of the match in extr -time. Paul Parker switched to the middle of the defence and played heroically alongside Des Walker, with Wright switching to right-back.

In the 14th minute of extra time Gascoigne stepped up the pace, just as he had against Belgium. He pushed a perfect pass through to Lineker, whose promising run towards goal was halted when goalkeeper Thomas Nkono pulled him down. With a coolness that was surely only an act, Lineker shot his penalty on a straight line into the net while Nkono was diving to his right snatching at empty air.

England had won a memorable match, and created history by becoming the first English team to reach the World Cup semi-finals on foreign soil. Their combination of luck and pluck had triumphed over the skills of a Cameroon team that had done their country and the continent of Africa proud.

 Saint comments

It defies logic that England are now within shooting distance of the World Cup final after being outplayed by Cameroon, who have really put African football on the map. But you will not find a pro who is not lost in admiration for the way England battled against heavy odds. It's all very well getting luck in football, but it takes a brave team to make the most of it. They don't come braver – or luckier – than England. Now let's see what they can do against West Germany. It looks a bridge too far to me.

Bobby Robson, England's manager: "It took resilience, spirit, determination and great morale to pull us through. Let's be honest and admit that Cameroon tore us apart at times. We never underestimated them, but they were even better than we thought. I had 19 heart attacks watching the game, but in the end true Brit grit won the game for us. Every player was a hero, but I have to single out Peter Shilton, Mark Wright and Paul Parker. They were magnificent. Cameroon have proved that African football is up there with the best. Now we must start planning for the semi-final against West Germany. The pressure will be on them because we shall be the underdogs. I just hope we can get all our walking wounded fit in time for the match."

Gary Lineker, scorer of two penalties for England: "I just kept telling myself to stay calm. As I waited to take the second penalty I found my thoughts drifting to my brother who I knew would be watching on television in Tenerife, where he is on holiday. He is always a bag of nerves when I play and I wondered how he was reacting. Then I got my concentration on the job in hand and made sure I hit the target. We battled hard for that victory against a team that could really play the game."

Roger Milla, Cameroon's World Cup hero: "I will change my mind about retiring, and will play on. We've shown that African football is as good as anywhere else in the world. Now we should be allowed more representative teams in the finals. England must know that it is Cameroon who deserved to go through. We were on top for most of the game, and we just cannot believe we lost after creating so many chances. At least the world now knows all about us and we have enjoyed ourselves."

Facing page: Eugene Ekeke stuns England with a goal for Cameroon

World Cup chat-a-thon

 So now we know the semi-finals line-up, Greavsie: Italy against Argentina and West Germany against, surprise, surprise, England. I'm predicting an Italy–West Germany final, but the way this World Cup has gone I would not be that astonished if we finished up with Argentina playing England. It's almost as if the footballing gods rather than the players are deciding the outcome of each match. Who are you tipping?

Well, I've been predicting a West Germany versus Italy final from before a ball was kicked, and I am going to stick with that. It would be justice if they were to meet in the final because they have been far and away the two best teams in the tournament. England have battled through to the last four by riding their luck and showing tremendous character, and Argentina have scrambled through without once looking the part of defending world champions.

I've detested the way Argentina have played in these finals, and I hope Italy give them a good thrashing in their semi-final. They have become spoilers and have concentrated on stopping the opposition playing with tactics that belong more in the professional wrestling ring than on the football pitch. That business of rolling around in mock agony to make ordinary tackles seem like GBH assaults is a disgrace.

I think we're agreed, Saint, that the referees have been hopeless in separating the actors from the genuine pros. Mind you, in fairness to the refs they don't have the advantage of watching an action replay to see that a player who has fallen down as if shot has in actual fact not been touched. The worst culprit has been Maradona, who should set standards only of greatness. He has allegedly been the most fouled player in the tournament. There is no

"A late news item – Cameroon have sacked their witch doctor because his magic potion guaranteeing good luck was delivered to the wrong dressing-room."

doubt that he has been heavily tackled on occasions, but too many times he has feigned being whacked. Like you, I would like to see Italy hammer them, but the match is being played at Diego's second home in Naples and he just might select this match to turn on one of his magical performances.

And how about England? You have to admit, Greavsie, that they are the luckiest team in the world to be in the semi-finals. I see the players are upset at being labelled lucky, but think how they would have felt if they had played as well as Cameroon and then found themselves out.

I can't argue with you on that one, Saint. But you have to admire the way England battled. There were no actors in our team. Now comes the big test. The formbook goes out the window when England play Germany. My heart hopes England win. My head says it must be Germany.

92

Tuesday July 3   Semi-final
Italy (1) **1,Argentina** (0) **1**
Naples *Argentina won 4–3 on penalties*

 Saint reports

Argentina chose this semi-final in which at last to get their act together and they wrecked Italy's grand dream of winning the World Cup in front of their own supporters in Rome. They did it in the cruellest possible manner, winning a nail-biting penalty shoot-out after the teams had finished deadlocked at 1–1 after extra time.

The belated arrival of Argentina looking the part of world champions coincided with the departure of Italy's nerve on the doorstep to the final. They snatched the lead against the run of play and then became gripped by fear, electing to try to sit on the lead rather than going all out to build on it.

This win by Argentina was, in my view, a defeat for football. Throughout the tournament they have been moody and petulant, and they have set the worst possible example of the spirit in which the game should be played. Now they have muddled through to the final after winning only one of their group matches and scraping through the quarter- and semi-finals on penalties.

What a tragedy for Italy. They were convinced it was their destiny to win the World Cup for a record fourth time. Along with West Germany they had the best team, but when it really mattered they did not have the right temperament. All their beautiful skills became stifled as the expectations of their supporters weighed on their backs like sacks of cement. Now the most they can hope for is to win the play-off for third place, and that will be dismissed as failure in a country in which football is a religion and where everybody was thinking only of winning the World Cup.

Argentina opened brightly and played their most inspiring football of the tournament in the first 15 minutes, but it was Italy who stole the lead in the 17th minute. And it was that man Salvatore "Toto" Schillaci, the most exciting discovery of the finals, who pounced to score his fifth goal in five matches. He started the goal-scoring movement with a neat pass to Giuseppe Giannini, and he transferred it to the recalled Gianluca Vialli whose powerful shot was only parried by goalkeeper Sergio Goycochea. It was Schillaci, looking off side to me, who was in the right place at the right time to ram the ball firmly into the net from close range.

That should have been the signal for Italy to unleash the full force of their attack, but old habits die hard and they retreated nervously into a defensive formation just like so many Italian teams in the past have done. This negative approach gave Argentina heart and hope, and suddenly they started to play as if they believed they could win the game. Diego Maradona was moved to make some probing runs from midfield that reminded us that he is much more than just a ham actor, and he gave us a flash of the Maradona of old with a savage shot on the turn that nearly caught goalkeeper Walter Zenga unawares. Ahead of Maradona the blond Claudio Caniggia was causing problems in the previously untroubled Italian defence with his aggressive sprints. Jorge Burruchaga and Jose Basualdo were pushing forward in support of Caniggia, and you could sense Italy's defence crumbling on the verge of a nervous breakdown.

It came in the 68th minute, and it was Maradona who was the author of the attack that had as its final chapter the first goal conceded by Italy in World Cup '90. He pushed the sweetest of passes out to Julio Olarticoechea, and his teasing cross caught Zenga in two minds as to whether to come off his line. During the first half Zenga had overtaken Peter Shilton's record for the longest spell without conceding a goal in World Cup matches, but his indecision was exposed as he elected, too late, to challenge for the ball. Cannigia beat him by a split second and back-headed the ball into the far corner of the net.

Now Italy were rocking on their heels. This was when they should have been raising their game as England had done against Belgium and Cameroon when they were in trouble, but when they put their foot on the accelerator

The save that plunged a nation into mourning. Sergio Goycoechea pounces to stop Roberto Donadoni's penalty

there was nothing there. Aldo Serena and Roberto Baggio were sent on as substitutes for Vialli and Giannini as manager Azeglio Vicini juggled his pack of star players, but panic had now set in and it was Argentina who were flourishing the thoughtful and creative football that had been an Italian copyright in this tournament.

When the match boiled over into extra time the Argentinians seemed so confident they could win a penalty shoot-out that they resorted to time-wasting tactics, and we were once again subjected to the sickening sight of players rolling around after tackles in their efforts to steal precious seconds. Maradona again showed his other ugly face as he won a free kick with an outrageous dive after the boot aimed at him had clearly missed its target. Then Ricardo Giusti stupidly got himself sent off for an off-the-ball duel with Roberto Baggio that finished with the world's most expensive footballer lying flat out holding his face.

Led by a demonstrative Maradona, a posse of protesting players surrounded the linesman who had drawn the referee's attention to the incident, and in what was almost an action replay of Antonio Rattin's sending-off against England in the 1966 quarter-finals it looked as if the Argentinians were going to refuse to play on. But, no doubt prompted by the fact that they could smell victory, common sense got the better of them.

The first period of extra time stretched an incredible eight minutes over the alloted 15 minutes, and in the second period Argentina's ten men comfortably held out to force a penalties showdown. As the final whistle blew Maradona punched the air in triumph as if he knew Argentina had booked their place in the final.

It was almost possible to hear Italian knees knocking as they huddled in the centre-circle waiting their turns to take the spot-kicks. Serrizuela netted the first penalty for Argentina, which was cancelled cut by a successful conversion by Baresi. Burruchaga and then De Agostini made it 2–2.

94

Olarticoechea made it 3–2 to Argentina before Roberto Donadoni, who had filled this World Cup with so many good moments, watched his feeble shot saved by goalkeeper Goycochea. Poor Donadoni fell to his knees like a man ready for the executioner's axe.

Next up it was Maradona. He strutted into the penalty area as if he owned the place (Naples pay him so much money to play there at club level that he possibly does). Diego is the only man I know who manages to be arrogant with a penalty kick. He made amends for his miss against Yugoslavia with a perfectly placed left-foot ground shot that he almost caressed into the net. Argentina 4, Italy 3.

Aldo Serena, who must have been wishing he had been left on the substitutes' bench, had to score to keep Italy alive in the World Cup. Goycochea, the second-string goalkeeper who came into the side after Nery Pumpido broke a leg in the group match against the Soviets, became Argentina's instant hero and broke millions of Italian hearts as he dived to his left to make a scrambled save.

Somehow Argentina had got themselves into the World Cup final. It's a sad old game, Greavsie. Ask any Italian.

 *Greavsie comments*

Let's not mince words. Italy bottled it. They ran out of belief in themselves in their moment of need. If they had played anything like the sort of attacking football with which they had lit up their earlier matches they would have run Argentina's defence ragged. But they were beaten by their nerves, and it was so obvious that they were in the grip of fear that it pumped new-found confidence into Argentina.

This was the worst possible result for the tournament. Italian interest in the proceedings will be greatly diminished, which means a lot of the Roman passion will be missing from the final. I felt desperately sorry for little Toto Schillaci. If ever a man deserved to be in a World Cup final it was the Sicilian hitman. Argentina will hardly come top of any popularity poll, but they could have the last laugh on the road to Rome.

Diego Maradona, Argentina's captain: "I knew we would beat Italy because I have had a dream of an Argentina–England final. And in my dream we win the Cup again. Whoever we meet in the final will have to tear the Cup from our hearts. We are determined not to let it go now that we have got this close to retaining it. I accept that we have had luck on our side on our way into the final, but we deserved the glory against Italy. This is my last World Cup. I am 30 now and I will not want to play in the 1994 tournament. I want to have the sweetest story to tell my grandchildren. For my dream to come true England must beat West Germany, and I shall be cheering them on. I may have looked cool when I took my penalty against Italy, but inside I was terrified. Goalkeeper Walter Zenga knows me and my game well. I was frightened that he was going to save my shot. We have tortured ourselves to reach this final. Now we must not let anybody stop us from winning it. I am half sad for Italy because it is my second country, but my first priority must be to try to help Argentina win the Cup again."

Azeglio Vicini, Italy's manager: "We tried to satisfy our fans in all our matches by attacking – and tonight we paid the price. We should have conserved our energy. My players just ran out of steam, and that is why we have missed out on what should have been a great moment in our history. The only thing the Argentinians were better at was penalty shooting. It is heart-breaking to lose like that."

Carlos Bilardo, manager of Argentina: "We have performed miracles getting to the final again because we have been troubled by so many injuries. Maradona has played in pain, and I have great admiration for his efforts. My worry now is finding four replacements for the players who will miss Sunday's final because of suspension. It will not be easy."

 *Greavsie reports*

England saved their finest performance of World Cup '90 for this epic semi-final, but they finished up with empty hands and broken hearts as the old enemy West Germany conquered them in yet another torturous penalty shoot-out. So now we have a repeat of the 1986 World Cup final, and both Argentina and West Germany have come to this return encounter across a bridge of penalties that has turned these championships into a frustrating lottery.

England produced what was probably the most impressive team display of Bobby Robson's eight-year reign, which is now just the third-place play-off match away from its conclusion before he returns to club football as manager of PSV Eindhoven. The players did Bobby and their country proud, and I suppose you could say they got to within 12 yards of the final. That's the distance of the spot-kicks that were to prove England's downfall in a dramatic duel that dragged at the emotions of players and spectators alike.

A 1–1 draw after extra time was just about a fair reflection on a masterpiece of a match in which both England and West Germany set an example of how football can be played with spirit and fire and without need to resort to petty fouling and theatrical falling.

Fussy refereeing and play-acting players have scarred these finals, but England and West Germany flourished football that was a feast for the eyes and always fiercely yet sportingly contested. There was just one irritating incident when Thomas Berthold made a meal of a tackle by Paul Gascoigne in extra time, and Gazza was close to tears as he collected his

Facing page: Terry Butcher takes a fatherly role as he tries to console the tearful Paul Gascoigne after England's penalties defeat

second booking of the tournament which would have ruled him out of the final.

Gascoigne has been one of *the* players of World Cup '90. He was more prominent and productive in midfield than West German skipper Lothar Matthaeus, who had been rated by many as the best player on view before this match. In the opening minutes of the most important match of his life Gazza had been confident and cheeky enough to try a long-range shot that forced an acrobatic save from goalkeeper Bodo Illgner.

England were unquestionably the sharper and more skilful side throughout most of the first half. Their formation was rearranged to allow Mark Wright, wearing a patch over his stitched left-eye injury, to play alongside Des Walker at the heart of the defence, with Terry Butcher dropping back as the free man. Peter Beardsley came in for injured John Barnes, and gave his brightest performance for several months. He supported in attack and beavered in midfield where Gascoigne and the assured David Platt were dictating the pace and pattern of the play. Gary Lineker foraged at the front with all his old sharpness and stealth, convincing me that we were watching the finest England striker of all time – yours truly included.

Chris Waddle was again at his tormenting best, and he had Illgner scurrying to tip over an impudent lob from close to the half-way line that was reminiscent of Pelé's famous effort in the 1970 World Cup finals. Paul Parker and Stuart Pearce were making adventurous runs down the flanks, and for the first time in the tournament the Germans were having to play at full throttle just to stay in the game.

Strangely, England began to lose some of their impetus after West Germany had watched their number one striker Rudi Voeller limp off with a leg injury in the 31st minute. Karlheinz Riedle came on as substitute and brought a new dimension to the attack, and his nippy style of play briefly disconcerted and disoriented England's three central defenders, who had been handling Juergen Klinsmann and Voeller with reasonable comfort.

Germany really got into their stride in the second half and Peter Shilton was called on to show what a magnificent last line of defence he is, even if he is still playing at a time when most footballers have hung up their boots and are thinking about their pensions.

Shilton was desperately unlucky to concede the first goal of the match in the 59th minute. Paul Parker dashed forward to try to block Andreas Brehme's shot after the Germans had been awarded a free kick in a central position 20 yards out. Shilton, collecting his 124th cap, had rightly come off his line to narrow the angle and was caught in no man's land as the ball deflected off Parker's heel and ballooned freakishly high before coming down first bounce into the back of England's net.

Tottenham team-mates Gascoigne and Lineker were first to respond in a positive way to this set back, and together they inspired the England players by raising their game to a new peak. Gazza very nearly created two goals out of nothing in the space of a couple of minutes with power-charged runs that had German defenders back-pedalling in panic.

Bobby Robson also reacted positively, sending on the neat and precise Trevor Steven to a midfield base as a replacement for the largely redundant Terry Butcher, who handed his captain's armband to Shilton.

England's reward for their tireless running and creative probing was a gem of a goal by Lineker in the 80th minute. He confused two accompanying German defenders with a darting run to meet a cross by the quick and clever Parker. He controlled the ball beautifully with his right thigh, pushing it out to his left and then hitting it in full stride with his left foot to send it under a sliding defender and into the far corner of the net. It was a goal of pure class and worthy of the setting of a World Cup final, let alone a semi-final.

Both Waddle and Guido Buchwald hammered shots against the post during a thrilling extra-time period before the game moved towards the almost inevitable challenge of penalties. England had produced a superhuman performance, but were looking tired and drained at the final whistle. They could give only so much, and remember that only three days earlier they had been locked in an extra-time battle with Cameroon.

It soon became evident that they had used up their full quota of luck against Cameroon.

Shilton elected the right way to dive for every one of the German penalties, but each time he was a fingernail's distance away from making a vital save. Lineker took the first penalty and coolly drilled it home. Brehme made it all square. Then Beardsley netted penalty number two, which was cancelled out by Matthaeus with the most ferocious spot-kick of the tournament. David Platt, growing in stature with every minute of these finals, made it 3–2 while Paul Gascoigne looked on from the centre-circle with tears watering his eyes. He was going through the mental torture of knowing that even if England won he was out of the final.

Riedle brought the scores level again before Stuart Pearce, who packs one of the hardest shots in football, took aim and fired the first blank. He was inconsolable as his low-driven spot-kick cannoned off Illgner's shins. Pearce has had an outstanding tournament, and did not deserve this cruel moment in his life.

Olaf Thon netted his next penalty, meaning that Chris Waddle had to hit the target to keep alive England's hopes of reaching the final. For the life of me I could not understand why Waddle had been nominated as one of England's five penalty takers. He admits he has never taken a spot-kick in a major match in his career, and he produced a novice-like effort as he blazed the ball high over the bar.

Germany were through to the final, but England went out with honour in a match that was a credit to the World Cup and to football in general.

 *Saint comments*

England's luck deserted them when they most needed it, but their performance restored faith in the quality of British football. It was hard for England to lose like this, but in all honesty it would have been even tougher on the Germans. They have consistently been the outstanding team in the tournament, and on their overall showing they thoroughly deserve their place in the final. Greavsie and I will be roaring them on against the Argentinians, who don't deserve to win an egg cup.

True sportsman Lothar Matthaeus takes time out from celebrating West Germany's victory to spare a word of sympathy for Chris Waddle following his penalty miss

QUOTE UNQUOTE

Bobby Robson, England's manager: "We're spilling tears by the bucketful. It's heartbreaking to go out when we were so close. We really fancied we could win it. Once we had got past the Germans we wanted to avenge our defeat by Argentina in the 1986 finals. We were so, so close. I hate these penalty shoot-outs, not just because we lost but because they are too cruel on the players. I can't understand why we just don't play on after the end of extra time until somebody scores. Change ends after each 15 minutes and carry on until the ball is put into one net or the other. It would be just as exciting as these penalty shoot-outs, but a lot fairer. Let me just say that I have never been prouder to be England manager than when I saw the effort our lads put in against Germany. We have shown the world that we can really play the game as well, if not better, than anybody. Let's stop knocking British football and start shouting from the rooftops that our game is in good shape. We have got some of the greatest young players in the world. Paul Gascoigne has been the best young player on show, and there's no end to what he can now achieve in the game. Then there are youngsters like Paul Parker, David Platt and Des Walker who are going to give marvellous service to England."

Franz Beckenbauer, West Germany's manager: "It was a great pity that either team had to lose in this way, but penalty shoot-outs are what the regulations say must decide a drawn game. England played magnificently, and gave us our hardest match of the tournament. Now we look forward to trying to beat Argentina in the final. I am confident we will because we are a better team than when we met four years ago, while I don't think they are the same force. We shall see."

Paul Gascoigne, England's midfield hero: "I'm too choked to be able to talk. I just hope nobody thinks we let them down. Nobody could have tried harder than we did to reach the final."

99

World Cup chat-a-thon

After all that, Greavsie, we've gone and finished up with a repeat of the 1986 final – Argentina against West Germany. All I hope is that it doesn't end with the same result because there is no way that Argentina can be held up as worthy world champions. They've scrambled through to the final on penalties. I know that Germany have got there by the same route, but at least they've played some quality football on the way to the final. Yet I have a feeling in my old bones that Argentina are going to steal a victory. They started to show just glimpses of their best in the semi-final against Italy.

Giller

"We will bring you our interview with young Paul Gascoigne just as soon as we've found another box of Kleenex."

I understand what you mean, but Germany should have too much all-round strength for them. We've been in the game long enough to know that form counts for nothing in the final. It's a one-off, and emotions and pride take over. Argentina have one of the most pedestrian sides they have ever sent to a World Cup, yet in Maradona they continue to have the ace in the pack. He has produced just hints that he is getting his old appetite and delicate touch back. It only needs him to turn it on in the final and it could wreck Franz Beckenbauer's chances of becoming the first man ever to have captained and managed World Cup-winning teams.

Apart from Gazza's tears, the major talking point as we wait for the third-place play-off and the final is the penalty shoot-out system for breaking match deadlocks. Do you think it's a fair way to decide which team goes through if the scores are level after extra time?

Let's face it, Saint, there isn't a fair way. No matter what you decide, the losing team is going to feel hard done by. At least the penalties system is fairer than what happened in our playing days when a coin was tossed to decide the winners.

Thank goodness they've tossed that out. I've advocated for a long time that corner kicks should be taken into consideration if the teams are level after extra time. The team that has forced most corners wins. The trouble with that, of course, is that the spectators feel cheated because, let's be frank, they get tremendous entertainment out of the Russian roulette penalty system. While all of us in the game are whingeing about the system, many of the people who really matter – the punters – seem to be really enjoying it and are talking about the penalties more than anything else.

It must be worth looking at the American way of deciding deadlocked matches. They've adapted the shoot-out idea used in ice hockey. A player runs towards goal from 35 yards and has to try to beat the goalkeeper who has the freedom to come off his line. There is certainly more footballing skill involved than in just a one-off blast at goal from the penalty spot.

Then there's the idea of Bobby Robson's that extra time should be extended by 15 minute periods until a team scores. Franz Beckenbauer has gone one step further by saying that if there

100

is still no end to the deadlock one or two players should be taken off the pitch at the end of every 15 minutes of extra extra time. This way a goal would have to come eventually.

The problem with all these ideas, Greavsie – and let's be brutally honest about this – is that television calls the tune in all major sports events these days. Can you imagine what it would do to programme schedules if a game went on and on without the deadlock being broken? And what concerns me about the idea of playing on through extra extra time is that it could do untold damage to any player carrying an injury. The substitutes would almost certainly have been used by then, and an injured player not wanting to let his team down might force himself to play on and cause all sorts of complications to the injury.

My bet is that the penalty system will still be with us for the 1994 World Cup in the United States. The American television executives loved what they called the PKs. It was about the only part of the game that many of them understood. They will see "Penalty Kicks" as a way to sell the finals to the American public.

One thing's for sure, Jim, we have not heard the last of the subject. Most people in the game are against the penalty system because it puts an unfair burden on individual players in what is essentially a team game. Poor old Stuart Pearce and, to a lesser extent Chris Waddle, are always going to be haunted by the moment when they failed to find the net in the semi-final shoot-out. It's a cruel way to ask players to end the deadlock, but it's a hit with the public. And at the end of the day we have to concede that football is part of the entertainment industry. All I hope is that the World Cup final is not decided by penalties. What I want to see is a a match full of top-quality football, and a game fit for the occasion without any temperamental nonsense or theatrical acting by players feigning injury. Most of all I want to see West Germany win, simply because they have consistently been the best team in the

"Another late news item for our two viewers – the Americans have suggested that for each game in the 1994 World Cup finals we start off with a penalty shoot-out and, if it is all square after ten penalties each, decide the winners by playing a match."

tournament. Yes, Greavsie, I know – you picked them to win before a ball was kicked.

That's nice of you, Saint, to remind our reader. But you didn't have to say it through gritted teeth. I am the world's worst tipster. As Ron Atkinson always tells me, I could not tip rubbish. Yet for some reason I always manage to get it right for the World Cup finals. I tipped Italy in 1982 and Argentina in 1986, and, incidentally, I also tipped England to win in 1966, but I didn't know they were going to do it without me! Anyway, before the big final we have the third-place play-off between England and Italy. That's a match the players could do without, but it would be nice to see England win just to put a smile back on Gazza's face and to give Bobby Robson a happy send-off.

Aye, Jim, it's a pretty meaningless game and a terrible anti-climax for players who desperately wanted to be in the final. I think Italy will win because they have the greater incentive in front of their own fans. Let's just hope it doesn't go to penalties!

101

Saint reports

Bobby Robson's last match as England manager and Peter Shilton's final game as England goalkeeper ended in a defeat by Italy that was partly self-inflicted, but which did nothing to lessen the impact that England have managed to make on World Cup '90.

Shilton, captain for the night as he stretched his world-record collection of caps to 125, confirmed immediately after an eventful game that he was retiring from the international football scene that he has graced for 20 years.

He will remember his farewell performance for all the wrong reasons. The man who has been one of the most reliable players in the history of English football made a calamitous mistake that cost England the match.

The third-place play-off is usually unwanted furniture cluttering the World Cup time table. But this one was surprisingly enjoyable thanks to the spirit in which it was played. Both sides were competitive in their attitude without being cut-throat, and they won the appreciation and applause of the fans for their sporting manner.

There was almost a party spirit running through the game, the flames of friendship being fanned by the England substitutes and reserves who – with the mischievous Paul Gascoigne leading the way – were doing their own version of the "Mexican Wave" on the touchline bench.

Bobby Robson resisted the temptation to give all his reserve players a run-out, and stuck fairly closely to his tried and tested team. Tony Dorigo came in at left-back for Chris Waddle, Steve McMahon took over from the suspended Paul Gascoigne, and Gary Stevens was recalled at right-back, with Paul Parker switching to sweeper. Mark Wright played a conventional central defensive role in place of Terry Butcher, another fine England

servant whose international career is now almost certainly over.

The game featured fast, skilful, end-to-end action missing only the final touch, and then Shilton made his fatal error in the 70th minute. The man renowned for his obsessive attention to detail was guilty for one of the few times in his career of losing his concentration. He had just taken possession of the ball and elected to roll it along the ground as he looked for an England player to whom he could pass it. Peter must have been the only person in the stadium who did not see Roberto Baggio loitering alongside him. Baggio must have thought Christmas had come early as Shilton virtually placed the ball at his feet. He turned it back into the path of Salvatore Schillaci as Shilts frantically chased around trying to retrieve the ball. Suddenly five England defenders were scurrying around the goalmouth like headless chickens as they attempted to block Schillaci's way to goal. He threaded the ball back to Baggio, who appeared to be off side. The £8 million golden boy of Italian football then dribbled his way across the face of the England goal before scoring with a close-range shot.

Just as the killer goal hit the back of England's net, Chris Waddle was preparing to come on as substitute for the injured Wright, who had been in phenomenal form and revived memories of Franz Beckenbauer at his best with his dribbling runs and precise passes from the back. Bobby Robson also sent Neil Webb on in place of Steve McMahon to join in yet another spirited England revival.

Ten minutes after Shilton's error the skilful Dorigo made an enterprising run down the left wing before sending over a measured cross. David Platt, who had been making penetrating bursts into the Italian penalty area throughout the game, powered the ball into the net from 12 yards for one of the best headed goals of the whole tournament.

Penalties have become such a part and parcel of these finals that it hardly came as a shock when Paul Parker was adjudged to have fouled Salvatore Schillaci when they became

Facing page: Patched-up Mark Wright shows Roberto Baggio why he was rated one of the finest defenders in the tournament

tangled in the penalty area in the 84th minute. Little Toto, needing one goal to become the leading marksman of World Cup '90, sent Shilton the wrong way as he drilled in his sixth goal of the finals to which he has made a huge personal contribution.

Shilton's magnificent international career had to survive one more embarrassing moment before he could bow out. Nicola Berti beat him with a looping header in the closing minutes, but as the great man turned to retrieve the ball from the net he was relieved to see the linesman's flag raised to signal off side.

England had lost, but their dignity and their pride were still intact. They deserved the standing ovation handed to them by the mainly Italian audience who had appreciated their part in an open and enjoyable match.

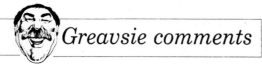 *Greavsie comments*

England officially finished fourth in the World Cup, but they were first in the eyes of many for the spirit with which they played the game. They functioned throughout with honest endeavour, and by the time they had got into their stride and rhythm in the later stages were producing some of the most eye-catching of all the football played.

You never saw England players feigning injury, or trying to get opponents booked by making tackles appear worse than they were. It was right and proper that they should have been elected winners of the prestigious "Fair Play" award.

Italy just deserved their victory, and if there had been any justice they would have been in the final. For them, this third place represented failure but – like England – they had won friends around the world with the quality of their football. One of the most heartening of all sights came after the final whistle when the players of both teams first of all joined in a spontaneous "Mexican Wave" and then shared a lap of honour. It will be a perfect finale if West Germany and Argentina can match the spirit and the sportsmanshp shown by both sides in what could have been a meaningless game. But somehow I doubt if they will.

Peter Shilton, England's goalkeeper: "I was guilty of a silly mistake, but I am not going to let it spoil what has been a memorable World Cup. It would have been fantastic to have won the tournament, a dream come true. But even if we had I would still have announced my decision to retire from international football. I've got a couple of years left on my contract with Derby County and will see that through before perhaps considering a player-manager's job. I told my family I would finish no matter what happened. I wanted to go out right at the top. I have loved every second of my career with England, but 20 years is a long time to play at this level and it's time I made way for one of the younger goalkeepers. I would like to see Chris Woods take my place. He deserves the chance and I think he would make a good job of it."

Bobby Robson, England's manager: "Peter has been one of the great goalkeepers of all time, and a wonderful inspiration to everybody in the England squad. I have nothing but respect and admiration for him. He has been a model professional. I'm sad that Peter and I could not have gone out together on a winning note, but we didn't get the breaks. With a little luck we could have beaten Italy, just as we might have beaten West Germany and gone into the final. But you have to accept what you get in football, and on the whole I am delighted with our performances in the World Cup. We have regained our pride in the eyes of the world. I am leaving the job with a little sadness but satisfied that things are in good shape for my successor."

Azeglio Vicini, Italy's manager: "Both teams can be proud of what they achieved in this third-place play-off. The match was a wonderful advertisement for football, and the players of both sides deserve all the credit. This is what the spirit of football should be all about."

World Cup '90: THE FINAL

 Saint and Greavsie *report*

The Editor instructed our intrepid duo each to compile a separate report on the World Cup final, but they were so disappointed and disillusioned by what they saw that they produced this joint condemnation.

Cry for me Argentina, and for every football follower throughout the world. You brought shame and disgrace to what should have been a glittering showcase of all that is best about our great game. I have never been so saddened and so angry after a football match. The final was like a kick in the groin for our game, and did untold damage to its image at a time when the sport needs all the good news it can get.

I share every ounce of your anger, Saint, and I would just add that West Germany must shoulder a lot of the blame for dragging the World Cup down into the sewer. Several of their players were guilty of what has been the curse of these finals – the over-acting aimed at making tackles seem worse than they are. The finger of derision has also got to be pointed at Mexican referee Edgardo Codesal Mendez. The refereeing has been poor, bordering on the pathetic throughout the tournament, and Señor Mendez managed to save the most erratic display for the final. A gynaecologist when he is not refereeing, Señor Mendez plumbed the depths with decisions that were in turn inconsistent, weak and, often, wrong.

This is supposed to be a report of the final, so we had better talk about the action. Not that there was much of it from the defending world champions, who seemed to decide right from the

Sunday July 8	The Final

West Germany (0) **1**, **Argentina** (0) **0**
Rome   *Attendance: 73,603*
The teams:
Argentina: Goycochea, Simon, Serrizuela, Ruggeri (sub: Monzon), Lorenzo, Sensini, Basualdo, Burruchaga (sub: Calderon), Troglio, Maradona, Dezotti.
West Germany: Illgner, Augenthaler, Kohler, Buchwald, Berthold (sub: Reuter), Haessler, Matthaeus, Littbarski, Brehme, Voeller, Klinsmann.
Referee: Edgardo Codesal Mendez (Mexico).
Scorer: Brehme (penalty).

start that their only way of hanging on to the title was to play for a draw and hope to win a third successive penalty shoot-out. There was an early indication of the way Argentina had elected to play when Gustavo Dezotti was booked after only six minutes for disputing a free kick following a foul on Littbarksi. I did not think it warranted what was Argentina's 20th booking of the tournament, and from then on the South Americans were convinced the referee was against them. Their brittle temperament had them perched on a tightrope as they continually registered dissent.

The only way the Argentinians were going to get into the game was if Maradona started to unwrap his unique skill. He had announced just before the kick-off that this would be his final international appearance. I expected him to try to go out with a bang, but it was much more of a whimper. Guido Buchwald marked him so tightly that he was often like a second skin,

A sadly historic moment as Pedro Monzon becomes the first player to get sent off in a World Cup Final

and he stopped a strangely subdued Maradona from making any sort of impact on the match. There was just one flash of Maradona magic moments before half-time when he found Dezotti with a marvellous pass from that educated left foot of his, but Dezotti – deputising for the suspended and sorely missed Claudio Caniggia – was not good enough to be able to make anything of it. Maradona put a free kick over the bar, and that was the sum total of Argentina's shots on goal as they stumbled through the worst performance ever witnessed in a World Cup final.

The Germans had proved themselves the masters of the long-range shots on their way to the final. They had scored five of the 15 goals struck from outside the penalty area, and it looked as if this was going to be the only way to break the deadlock as the Argentinians packed players in their half of the field. No fewer than 16 shots flew from German boots to the one from Argentina, but they were rarely accurate enough or powerful enough to cause great concern to

goalkeeper Sergio Goycochea, who is one of the few Argentinians who can feel satisfied with his contribution to the World Cup. Lothar Matthaeus was bossing the match from midfield with a mixture of hard graft and creative skill, but twin strikers Rudi Voeller and Juergen Klinsmann were not responding to his intelligent prompting. Both of them, and in particular Klinsmann, seemed too intent on spending their energy trying to win penalties and free kicks by dramatic dives than concentrating on the job of banging the ball into the net.

Considering they were the two biggest men on the pitch, I could not believe the way Voeller and Klinsmann kept going down as if clobbered by Mike Tyson. I could understand Argentina's frustration, but they lost any sympathy they might have had by their petulant beha-

106

viour every time a decision went against them. Both Voeller and Klinsmann were involved in second-half flashpoints. Voeller was booked following a trip on Maradona, and then in the 65th minute Klinsmann made one of those high-tariff dives in which he specialises after being on the receiving end of a reckless tackle by Pedro Monzon. It was more clumsy than vicious, but Klinsmann's twisting fall was so dramatic that Señor Mendez was moved to become the first referee ever to send off a player in a World Cup final.

Monzon had only been on the pitch for 19 minutes as a substitute before he got into the record books in the worst possible way. His tackle was not that bad, but he was paying the price for all the sneaky and cynical fouls the Argentinians had been dishing out before his arrival. I have to agree with Jimmy and say that Klinsmann made it seem much worse than it was, and he deserved at least to have had his name taken for his constant diving. Just as we were dreading the prospect of extra time and the likelihood of yet another penalty shoot-out, West Germany stole the winner in the 85th minute, and – almost inevitably – it came from the penalty spot.

You chose the right word when you said "stole" the winner, Saint. The penalty should never have been awarded. Minutes earlier Señor Mendez had turned down legitimate appeals from the Argentinians for a penalty, and Latin blood boiled when he then pointed to the spot as Voeller went into yet another theatrical dive after falling over the outstretched foot of Nestor Lorenzo. Pedro Troglio was booked as angry Argentinian players surrounded the referee protesting against the harsh penalty award. Andreas Brehme, one of the tournament's outstanding players, slotted in the penalty, and the German players celebrated by performing victory rolls on top of each other. Not a pretty sight. There is no question that West Germany deserved to be in the lead, but the manner in which they got the goal that gave them revenge for their defeat by Argentina in the 1986 World Cup final was far from satisfactory.

Far too late, Argentina abandoned their negative attitude and started to play with urgency. When they were awarded a free kick Juergen Kohler went walk-about with the ball in his hands in a bid to buy time. Quite understandably, Dezotti wanted to get on with the game and he tried to wrestle the ball out of Kohler's grasp. Then, his temper in orbit, he wrestled Kohler to the ground. He had been booked in the first half, and so had to leave the pitch when the referee raised the red card. I could not see that Señor Mendez had any option, but he should also have at least booked Kohler for his time-wasting tactics that caused Dezotti's moment of madness.

Señor Mendez's red card was like a red cape to the Agentinians. It was shades of 1966 and the Antonio Rattin sending-off at Wembley again, and for a moment I thought they were going to lose the match on a default with the referee having no alternative but to abandon play. At the peak of their jostling, arm-waving protests skipper Maradona was booked. What a tragic way for him to finish what has, in all fairness, been an exceptional international career. These were shameful scenes, and the sickening thing is that millions of youngsters will have watched the shambles on television. What an example to set them. Argentina should be barred from international football until they learn how to behave. English clubs are punished because of the conduct of their fans. Argentina should pay for the petulance and spite of their players.

This is where we came in, Jim. The very first match of the tournament finished with nine men against eleven. Argentina against Cameroon. That match seems as if it was a year ago. What a disastrous end to World Cup '90. I feel sorry for Franz Beckenbauer. His crowning glory in his last match as West Germany's manager has been sabotaged by the behaviour of the Argentinian players. The game was an absolute disgrace, but Germany deserve to have won the World Cup for a record-equalling third time in their history because of the quality of their performances throughout the finals.

107

Was he pushed or did he fall? Rudi Voeller sprawls in the penalty area to earn the spot-kick that won the World Cup for West Germany

QUOTE UNQUOTE

Franz Beckenbauer, West Germany's manager: "I thought that we played an excellent game. It's a pity that Argentina did not seem to want to participate. They just tried to destroy the game. It was not an excellent match, but we are very satisfied with our performance. Argentina played a negative match, but that was not our fault. To have won 1–0 by a penalty falsifies the game. If we had won 3–0 that would have told the story. There were never any dangerous situations created by the Argentinians. We have had a magnificent tournament. From first match to last we have played at the highest level. The final was disappointing, but the important thing is that we have won."

Diego Maradona, who was in tears at the end: "I will have to tell my children that the mafia exists also in soccer. The penalty that beat us did not exist. It was given to award victory to West Germany and to punish Argentina. I cried not because we lost, but because of our impotence to fight superior forces that were stronger than West Germany. I have played my last game for Argentina. The time has come to hand over my captain's armband."

Carlos Bilardo, who was also having his last match as manager before returning to his job as a doctor: "It is not my policy to criticise referees. I leave it to others to draw their own conclusions. Our players are very upset, and with good reason. I have had to calm them down. Everybody saw what happened. You judge whether it was logical to have awarded a penalty. "

World Cup '90 trivia

●Don't mention "lucky 13th" to Argentine first-choice goalkeeper Nery Pumpido. In the 13th game of Italia '90 between Argentina and the Soviet Union on June 13, Pumpido broke his leg in a collision with team-mate Juan Simon. The collision occurred ten minutes into the game, but superstitious Argentinian journalists reported that it was 13 minutes after the kick-off when the luckless Pumpido was stretchered off.

●Argentina were the most superstitious side in the tournament. Midfield star Jorge Burruchaga was banned from shaving by his team-mates after he had scored Argentina's second goal in their win over the Soviet Union. Forward Pedro Troglio sprinkled grass from the pitch over his head for luck before each game. Their luck ran out in the final. Burruchaga was substituted and Troglio was booked. During the penalty shoot-out against Yugoslavia in the quarter-final one of the Argentine trainers took a small crucifix from his wallet and kissed it more than 50 times.

●The strict diet planning that normally accompanies a World Cup campaign became a thing of the past (or pasta) in Italia '90. Team doctors and physicians from several nations ordered their players to eat as much pasta and sugar as they could hold to counter-act the dehydration and energy-loss problems encountered during matches played in intense heat.

●England's kick-and-rush struggle against the Republic of Ireland in Italia '90 was heavily criticised by the Italian press. The country's leading sports newspaper *Gazzetta Dello Sport* ran the headline: NO FOOTBALL PLEASE – WE'RE ENGLISH!

●All football fans were given a chance to own part of the pitch at the Olympic Stadium in Rome. Following the Final, the pitch was cut up and sold at £100 for each small square.

"After the dung that West Germany and Argentina dropped on it in the final, it should be great on which to grow roses," said Greavsie.

●When the skies opened and the rains fell at Italia '90, true football fans must have cursed hooligans in dozens of tongues. Umbrellas were considered to be dangerous weapons and were banned from all grounds, leaving spectators to brave the Italian summer storms without protection.

● The finals had a world-wide audience of 31 billion viewers. More than half the world's population watched at least one match. Football fans in Thailand were not impressed with their coverage. Viewers had to sit through 40 commercial breaks during each match.

●*Tribune*, the best-selling newspaper in Cameroon, has launched a nationwide campaign to persuade the government to build a statue of 38-year-old World Cup hero Roger Milla in the centre of the capital Yaounde.

●Italian manager Azeglio Vicini must have wished he could have called on the services of veteran World Cup hero Paolo Rossi as his team struggled to find the net against Argentina. On the eve of the semi-final, Rossi, top scorer in the 1982 finals, hit the back of the net four times for a Europe select side against an Americas team in a veterans' charity match in Rome. Europe won 10–7, with Bobby Charlton scoring from the penalty spot against an Americas team that included such legends as Pele, Zico and Roberto Rivelino.

●The United Arab Emirates may not have won a game, but two of their players had reason to celebrate their World Cup campaign. Khalid Ismail Mubarak and Ali Thani Juma were both given Rolls Royce cars by an oil sheikh as reward for scoring the Emirates' only goals of the tournament.

●Jack Charlton's mother, Cissie, won £350 after placing a bet with Ladbrokes, correctly forecasting the Republic of Ireland's 1–1 draw with England. Mrs Charlton donated her winnings to a local school.

●Spain can claim to have the most dedicated fan of Italia '90 in Majorca bar owner Ramon Muzo. He cycled 1,100 miles from his home to watch Spain play South Korea in Udine, and then followed them to Verona for their next two matches.

●Italian magazine Novella 2000 staged a poll to find the best-looking and ugliest players in Italia '90. Striker Roberto Baggio was voted the most handsome, while one Diego Maradona was voted the least attractive.

●The makers of the table football game Subutteo received hundreds of requests from young fans for teams to be made up in the colours of Cameroon. They were voted the most colourful team in the tournament, and sportswear manufacturers are rushing Cameroon-colour kits into the shops.

●The Cameroon players were weighed down with good luck charms given to them by witch doctors, who were forbidden from treating any injured players in case they broke FIFA's strict laws on the use of drugs. There has been concern about the depth of the infuence of witch doctors on African football since a group of Zimbabwean players were banned for life after taking part in a ritual just before a match. They urinated in unison on the pitch.

●While things ran like a well-oiled engine on the pitch for West German manager Franz Beckenbauer, he had his troubles off the field. While he was plotting tactics for the second round match against Holland, a car thief drove off in his £70,000 Mercedes.

●Brazil's game against Sweden was in danger of being sabotaged until the World Cup organisers settled an outstanding bill. The firm that laid the turf at the Turin stadium were threatening to seize back the grass right up until they got paid just 24 hours before the kick-off.

●The biggest riot of the World Cup took place not in Sicily, but in India. Hundreds of football followers in Calcutta marched on the government electrical power headquarters and attacked department officials after power cuts had blacked out televised World Cup action.

●There was a strange slapping sound accompanying the play during Italy's second-phase match against Uruguay in Rome's Olympic Stadium. A swarm of gnats descended on the stadium just before the kick-off and spectators spent the entire match trying to slap the bloodthirsty insects as they continually landed on human flesh.

●The Dutch post office were licked along with Holland's players when they were eliminated by West Germany. They had ambitiously printed in advance of the match the first one million stamps of a special 16-million issue to mark a Dutch victory in the tournament. The million stamps, carrying the inscription "Netherlands World Champions 1990", were scrapped. "Sounds like they gummed up the works," said the Saint. "I wonder if they played the last post?" said Greavsie.

●Pope John Paul cut short his appointments on the day of Italy's match against Austria. "I must not stop the nation's duty of sitting in front of the television watching the football," explained his Holiness, a follower of the game who said, when introduced to Jack Charlton during the Republic of Ireland's audience at the Vatican, "Oh yes, you're the boss."

●The greyhound meeting at Wolverhampton was cancelled on the Monday that England played the Republic of Ireland. "Steve Bull could be playing," said a spokesman. "We can't compete with that."

●Reinhold Messner, one of Europe's leading mountaineers, keeps yaks as pets to remind him of his Everest climbs. He has renamed one of his yaks "Toto". "The yak has the same fiery eyes and spirit as Schillaci," explained Messner. Schillaci came top of an Italian poll to find the most popular World Cup player, with Franco Baresi second.

World Cup '90 dream team

The Editor asked Saint and Greavsie to each select a dream team from all the players that they have watched during World Cup '90, plus five substitutes. They did not confer before making the following selections:

SAINT'S TEAM
Formation: 1-4-3-2

Peter Shilton (England)

Franco Baresi (Italy)

Jorginho (Brazil)

Predrag Spasic (Yugoslavia)

Des Walker (England)

Andreas Brehme (W. Germany)

Dragan Stojkovic (Yugoslavia)

Lothar Matthaeus (W. Germany)

Gheorghe Hagi (Romania)

Salvatore Schillaci (Italy)

Gary Lineker (England)

GREAVSIE'S TEAM
Formation: 1-4-3-2

Peter Shilton (England)

Franco Baresi (Italy)

Andre Kana Biyick (Cameroon)

Giuseppe Bergomi (Italy)

Des Walker (England)

Andreas Brehme (W. Germany)

Dragan Stojkovic (Yugoslavia)

Lothar Matthaeus (W. Germany)

Paul Gascoigne (England)

Salvatore Schillaci (Italy)

Gary Lineker (England)

Subs: David Platt (England), **Roger Milla** (Cameroon), **Robert Prosinecki** (Yugoslavia), **Enzo Scifo** (Belgium), **Paul Gascoigne** (England).

Subs: Roger Milla (Cameroon), **Gheorghe Hagi** (Romania), **Alemao** (Brazil), **Giuseppe Giannini** (Italy), **Paul Parker** (England).

World Cup '90: The verdict

 Well, James, it's time for us to deliver our final findings on World Cup '90. We've seen 52 matches, 115 goals, a record 16 sendings-off and 170 bookings. The Editor has asked us to be judge and jury, and to come up with a verdict on the overall tournament.

 I'll tell you one thing, Saint, that Irish jig really suits you. Mind you, you look more like Wilfred Pickles than Judge Pickles. Yes, I know this is not the time to joke around, but I'm just trying to duck the issue because what I have to say might singe your wig. In a word I thought World Cup '90 was rubbish.

 I don't think you can dismiss it in one word. Let's be fair, there were some good moments. For a start, England and the Republic of Ireland came out of it well. We went in a bit strong on them after their opening game, but reflecting on it I think we can safely say that our football is not trailing light years behind the rest of the world like we thought in the opening stages of the finals.

 I'll go along with that, but the overall tournament was a massive disappointment. There were so many ham actors out on the pitches that the finals should have been organised by Equity rather than FIFA. You could count the truly world-class players on the fingers of Venus de Milo. I'm talking about players in the mould of Pele, Garrincha, Puskas, Cruyff, Beckenbauer. I could go on and on. What the tournament desperately needed was an outstanding Final to save it from being just about the least inspiring World Cup of all time. And look what we got – a match that dragged football into the gutter. Sorry, Saint, but my verdict on the World Cup is that it stank.

 You're obviously in the mood to be a hanging judge, Jim. Let's try to look at the positive things. West Germany played some superb football up until the Final, and Italy looked a magnificent team until they ran out of ideas against Argentina. I'll grant you there was nobody meeting the standards of the Peles and the Cruyffs, but the likes of Matthaeus, Stojkovic and Hagi provided some magical moments. I've not seen a better defender than Franco Baresi, and Toto Schillaci at times looked sensational. And what about the element of fun and surprise injected by Cameroon?

 If it had not been for Cameroon the finals would have been totally forgettable. Their opening victory over Argentina gave the World Cup the best possible kick-off, but the finals went downhill from then on. The main fault lay with the referees. They were so quick on the draw with their yellow cards that games lacked rhythm and flow. I honestly think the time has come to consider experimenting with a two-referee system. So much was being missed by the referee and his linesmen that they were causing more problems on the pitch than the players. How can we still have amateur referees in this day and age of ultra-professionalism? It's a joke.

 The biggest disappointment for me was the failure of Brazil to make any sort of impact. I think we would have had a much more open and enjoyable climax to the tournament if they had beaten Argentina in the second phase. The Argentinians were the luckiest team ever to reach the Final. They were certainly the victims of some atrocious refereeing against West Germany, but how can you have any sympathy for them? Throughout the tournament they were guilty of petulant and cynical behaviour, and they were never able to shake off a negative attitude apart from in the semi-final against Italy. If you think back to the 1986 finals they were virtually a one-man team then, and that one man was Maradona at his brilliant best. In World Cup '90 the wee man could hardly raise a gallop. He got a lot of close attention from defenders, and took more than his fair share of stick but that was no excuse for his devious tricks and dives.

 I see that I've dragged you down into my miserable mood. Let's try to end this journey through World Cup '90 on an optimistic note. The most encouraging thing of all was the performance of England after their dodgy start against the Republic of Ireland. They had the character to ride their luck against Belgium and Cameroon, and their displays against Holland, West Germany and Italy were among the most impressive in the entire tournament. The happiest Englishman in Italy must have been Graham Taylor because as the new England manager he is inheriting some exceptional players in Paul Parker, Des Walker, David Platt, Mark Wright and, of course, the most exciting of them all, Paul Gascoigne. He has a great foundation on which to build a challenge for the World Cup in the United States in 1994.

 So it was not all gloom and doom. The sweeper system was introduced with such great effect that it could bring a revolution in the way the game is played in Britain, and while we're talking about encouraging things let's praise the fans – particularly the Scots and the Irish – for their behaviour. Everybody was expecting the worst from the English supporters, but apart from some isolated incidents they came out of the finals with credit.

 You're so right, Saint. In fact the English fans brought fun rather than fear to the grounds, and their 'Let's-all have-a dis-co' dance and chants introduced a party spirit that could prove the way ahead for English football. Wouldn't it be great if we could spread that party mood right through the game.

SAINT & GREAVSIE'S WORLD CUP OSCARS

BEST ACTOR: We have a tie between Diego Maradona and Juergen Klinsmann, both of whom have perfected the theatrical dive. They continually fooled referees with their acting ability.

BEST TEAM: The award goes to Cameroon for bringing excitement, style and entertainment to the World Cup stage. They were desperately unlucky not to reach the semi-finals, and have put African football right on the map.

BEST PLAYER: Lothar Matthaeus, who was outstanding for West Germany in every match except the semi-final against England when he was overshadowed by Paul Gascoigne.

BEST NEWCOMER: Paul Gascoigne, who went into the finals a boy and came out a man. He is now a gold-plated superstar of English football, and provided he manages to keep his sense of fun can light up the world stage for years to come.

BEST DEFENDER: Italian sweeper Franco Baresi, who hardly put a foot wrong throughout the tournament and deserved a first-place rather than third-place medal. England had two outstanding challengers for this award in Mark Wright and Des Walker.

BEST STRIKER: Salvatore Schillaci, who was unknown outside Italy before the tournament started and finished up top marksman with six goals. His main challengers were Cameroon's crafty old Roger Milla and England's Gary Lineker.

BEST GOALKEEPER: Peter Shilton, despite his ghastly error in the third-place match against Italy. He has been a magnificent servant to England.

BEST MATCH: A tie between West Germany's games against England and Holland.

World Cup '90: The final count

Facts and figures collated by Michael Giller

All the men and the matches that mattered leading to this...

Austria   Italy   Czech.   USA

Austria Runners-up Europe Group 3		**Italy** Host Nation	**Czech.** Runners-up Europe Group 7		**USA** Runners-up North & Central America	
USSR v Austria	2–0	Italy automatically qualified for the finals as the host nation.	Luxembourg v Czech.	0–2	Costa Rica v USA	1–0
Austria v Turkey	3–2		Czech. v Belgium	0–0	USA v Costa Rica	1–0
E. Germany v Austria	1–1		Belgium v Czech.	2–1	USA v T'dad/Tobago	1–1
Iceland v Austria	0–0		Czech. v Luxembourg	4–0	USA v Guatemala	2–1
Austria v Iceland	2–1		Switzerland v Czech.	0–1	El Salvador v USA	0–1
Austria v USSR	0–0		Czech. v Portugal	2–1	Guatemala v USA	0–0
Turkey v Austria	3–0		Czech. v Switzerland	3–0	USA v El Salvador	0–0
Austria v E. Germany	3–0		Portugal v Czech.	0–0	T'dad/Tobago v USA	0–1

Manager: Josef Hickersberger *Squad:*	*Manager:* Azeglio Vicini *Squad:*	*Manager:* Josef Venglos *Squad:*	*Manager:* Bob Gansler *Squad:*
1. Klaus Lindenberger	1. Walter Zenga	1. Jan Stejskal	1. Tony Meola
2. Ernst Aigner	2. Franco Baresi	2. Julius Bielik	2. Steve Trittschuh
3. Robert Pecl	3. Giuseppe Bergomi	3. Miroslav Kadlec	3. John Doyle
4. Anton Pfeffer	4. Luigi de Agostini	4. Ivan Hasek	4. Jimmy Banks
5. Peter Schoettel	5. Ciro Ferrara	5. Jan Kocian	5. Mike Windischmann
6. Manfred Zsak	6. Riccardo Ferri	6. Frantisek Straka	6. John Harkes
7. Kurt Russ	7. Paolo Maldini	7. Michal Bilek	7. Tab Ramos
8. Peter Artner	8. Pietro Vierchowod	8. Josef Chovanec	8. Brian Bliss
9. Anton Polster	9. Carlo Ancelotti	9. Lubos Kubik	9. Chris Sullivan
10. Manfred Linzmaier	10. Nicola Berti	10. Tomas Skuhravy	10. Peter Vermes
11. Alfred Hoertnagl	11. Fernando de Napoli	11. Lubomir Moravcik	11. Eric Wynalda
12. Michael Baur	12. Stefano Tacconi	12. Peter Fieber	12. Paul Krumps
13. Andreas Ogris	13. Giuseppe Giannini	13. Jiri Nemec	13. Eric Eichmann
14. Gerhard Rodax	14. Giancarlo Marocchi	14. Vladimir Weiss	14. John Stollmeyer
15. Christian Keglevits	15. Roberto Baggio	15. Vladimir Kinier	15. Des Armstrong
16. Andreas Reisinger	16. Andrea Carnevale	16. Viliam Hyravy	16. Bruce Murray
17. Heimo Pfeifenberger	17. Roberto Donadoni	17. Ivo Knoflicek	17. Marcelo Balboa
18. Michael Streiter	18. Roberto Mancini	18. Milan Luhovy	18. Kasey Keller
19. Gerald Glatzmayer	19. Salvatore Schillaci	19. Stanislav Griga	19. Chris Henderson
20. Andreas Herzog	20. Aldo Serena	20. Vaclav Nemecek	20. Paul Caligiuri
21. Michael Konsel	21. Gianluca Vialli	21. Ludek Miklosko	21. Neil Covone
22. Otto Konrad	22. Gianluca Pagliuca	22. Peter Paluch	22. David Vanole

Group B *Venues: Bari / Naples*

USSR Argentina Romania Cameroon

Winners Europe Group 3	**Defending Champions**	**Winners Europe Group 1**	**Winners Africa Group C**

USSR	Argentina	Romania	Cameroon
Iceland v USSR 1–1	Argentina automatically	Bulgaria v Romania 1–3	Cameroon v Angola 1–1
USSR v Austria 2–0	qualified for the	Romania v Greece 3–0	Gabon v Cameroon 1–3
USSR v E. Germany 3–0		Greece v Romania 0–0	Nigeria v Cameroon 2–0
Turkey v USSR 0–1	finals as the	Romania v Bulgaria 1–0	Angola v Cameroon 1–2
USSR v Iceland 1–1	defending champions.	Denmark v Romania 3–0	Cameroon v Gabon 2–1
Austria v USSR 0–0		Romania v Denmark 3–1	Cameroon v Nigeria 1–0
E. Germany v USSR 2–1			**Play-off**
USSR v Turkey 2–0			Cameroon v Tunisia 2–0
			Tunisia v Cameroon 0–1

Manager:
Valeri Lobanovski
Squad:
1. Rinat Dasayev
2. Vladimir Bessonov
3. Vagiz Khidiatullin
4. Oleg Kuznetsov
5. Anatolli Demianenko
6. Vasily Rats
7. Sergei Aleinikov
8. Genadi Litovchenko
9. Alexander Zavarov
10. Oleg Protasov
11. Igor Dobrovolski
12. Alexander Borodiuk
13. Akhrik Tsveiba
14. Vladimir Liutyi
15. Ivan Yeremchuk
16. Viktor Chanov
17. Andrei Zygmantovich
18. Igor Shalimov
19. Sergei Fokin
20. Sergei Gorlukovich
21. Valeri Broshin
22. Alexander Uvarov

Manager:
Carlos Bilardo
Squad:
1. Nery Pumpido
2. Sergio Daniel Batista
3. Abel Balbo
4. Jose Basualdo
5. Edgardo Bauza
6. Gabriel Calderon
7. Jorge Burruchaga
8. Claudio Caniggia
9. Gustavo Dezotti
10. Diego Maradona
11. Nestor Fabbri
12. Sergio Goycochea
13. Nestor Lorenzo
14. Ricardo Giusti
15. Pedro Monzon
16. Julio Olarticoechea
17. Roberto Sensini
18. Jose Serrizuela
19. Oscar Ruggeri
20. Juan Simon
21. Pedro Troglio
22. Fabian Cancelarich

Manager:
Emerich Jenei
Squad:
1. Silviu Lung
2. Mircea Rednic
3. Michael Klein
4. Ioan Andone
5. Iosif Rotariu
6. Gheorghe Popescu
7. Marius Lacatus
8. Ovidiu Sabau
9. Rodion Camataru
10. Gheorghe Hagi
11. Danut Lupu
12. Bogdan Stelea
13. Adrian Popescu
14. Florian Raducioiu
15. Dorian Mateut
16. Daniel Timofte
17. Ilie Dumitrescu
18. Gavril Balint
19. Emil Sandoi
20. Zsolt Musznay
21. Ionut Lupescu
22. Gheorghe Liliac

Manager:
Valeri Nepomniachi
Squad:
1. Joseph-Antoine Bell
2. Andre Kana Biyick
3. Denis Onana Jules
4. Benjamin Massing
5. Bertin Ebwelle Ndingue
6. Emmanuel Kunde
7. Francois Omam Biyick
8. Emile Mbouh Mbouh
9. Roger Milla
10. Louis-Paul Mfede
11. Eugene Ekeke
12. Alphonse Ayakan
13. Jean-Claude Pagal
14. Stephen Tataw Eta
15. Thomas Libiih
16. Thomas N'kono
17. Victor Ndip Akem
18. Bonaventure Djonkep
19. Roger Feutmba
20. Cyrille Makanaky
21. Kessack Maboang
22. Celestin Songo'o

Group C

Venues: Turin / Genoa

Scotland	Brazil	Sweden	Costa Rica
Runners-up Europe Group 5	**Winners South America Group 3**	**Winners Europe Group 2**	**Winners North & Central America**

Norway v Scotland	1–2	Venezuela v Brazil	1–3	England v Sweden	0–0	Guatemala v Costa Rica	1–0
Scotland v Yugoslavia	1–1	Chile v Brazil	1–1	Albania v Sweden	1–2	Costa Rica v Guatemala	2–1
Cyprus v Scotland	2–3	Brazil v Venezuela	6–0	Sweden v Poland	2–1	Costa Rica v USA	1–0
Scotland v France	2–0	Brazil v Chile	2–0	Sweden v England	0–0	USA v Costa Rica	1–0
Scotland v Cyprus	2–1			Sweden v Albania	3–1	T'dad/Tob. v Costa Rica	1–1
Yugoslavia v Scotland	3–1			Poland v Sweden	0–2	Costa Rica v T'dad/Tob.	1–0
France v Scotland	3–0					El Salvador v Costa Rica	2–4
Scotland v Norway	1–1					Costa Rica v El Salvador	1–0

Scotland	Brazil	Sweden	Costa Rica
Manager:	*Manager:*	*Manager:*	*Manager:*
Andy Roxburgh	Sebastiao Lazaroni	Olle Nordin	Bora Milutinovic
Squad:	*Squad:*	*Squad:*	*Squad:*
1. Jim Leighton	1. Claudio Taffarel	1. Sven Andersson	1. Gabelo Conejo
2. Alex McLeish	2. Jorginho	2. Jan Eriksson	2. Vladimir Quesada
3. Roy Aitken	3. Ricardo Gomez	3. Glenn Hysen	3. Roger Flores
4. Richard Gough	4. Dunga	4. Peter Larsson	4. Ronald Gonzalez
5. Paul McStay	5. Alemao	5. Roger Ljung	5. Marvin Obando
6. Maurice Malpas	6. Branco	6. Roland Nilsson	6. Jose Carlos Chavez
7. Mo Johnston	7. Bismarck	7. Niclas Nyhlen	7. Hernan Medford
8. Jim Bett	8. Valdo	8. Stefan Schwarz	8. German Chavarria
9. Ally McCoist	9. Careca	9. Leif Engqvist	9. Alexander Guimaraes
10. Murdo MacLeod	10. Silas	10. Klas Ingesson	10. Oscar Ramirez
11. Gary Gillespie	11. Romario	11. Ulrik Jansson	11. Claudio Jara
12. Andy Goram	12. Acacio	12. Lars Eriksson	12. Roger Gomez
13. Gordon Durie	13. Jose Mozer	13. Anders Limpar	13. Miguel Davis
14. Alan McInally	14. Aldair	14. Joakim Nilsson	14. Juan Cayasso
15. Craig Levein	15. Muller	15. Glenn Stroemberg	15. Roland Marin
16. Stuart McCall	16. Bebeto	16. Jonas Thern	16. Jose Jaikel
17. Stewart McKimmie	17. Renato	17. Tomas Brolin	17. Roy Mayers
18. John Collins	18. Mazinho	18. Johnny Ekstroem	18. Geovany Jara
19. David McPherson	19. Ricardo Rocha	19. Mats Gren	19. Hector Marchena
20. Gary McAllister	20. Tita	20. Mats Magnusson	20. Mauricio Montero
21. Robert Fleck	21. Mauro Galvao	21. Stefan Pettersson	21. Hermidio Barrantes
22. Bryan Gunn	22. Ze Carlos	22. Thomas Ravelli	22. Miguel Segura

Group D   *Venues: Bologna / Milan*

Yugoslavia   W. Germany   Colombia   UAE

Winners Europe Group 5	**Runners-up Europe Group 4**	**Winners South America Group 2**	**Runners-up East & West Asia**
Scotland v Yugoslavia 1–1	Finland v W. Germany 0–4	Colombia v Ecuador 2–0	UAE v N. Korea 0–0
Yugoslavia v France 3–2	W. Germany v Holland 0–0	Paraguay v Colombia 2–1	China v UAE 1–2
Yugoslavia v Cyprus 4–0	Holland v W. Germany 1–1	Ecuador v Colombia 0–0	S. Arabia v UAE 0–0
France v Yugoslavia 0–0	Wales v W. Germany 0–0	Colombia v Paraguay 2–1	UAE v Qatar 1–1
Norway v Yugoslavia 1–2	W. Germany v Finland 1–2		UAE v S. Korea 1–1
Yugoslavia v Scotland 3–1	W. Germany v Wales 2–1	**Play-off**	
Yugoslavia v Norway 1–0		Colombia v Israel 1–0	
Cyprus v Yugoslavia 1–2		Israel v Colombia 0–0	

Manager:	*Manager:*	*Manager:*	*Manager:*
Ivica Osim	Franz Beckenbauer	Francisco Maturana	Carlos Alberto Parriera
Squad:	*Squad:*	*Squad:*	*Squad:*
1. Tomislav Ivkovich	1. Bodo Illgner	1. Rene Higuita	1. Abdullah Moosa
2. Vujadin Stanojkovic	2. Stefan Reuter	2. Andres Escobar	2. Khaleel G. Mubarak
3. Predrag Spasic	3. Andreas Brehme	3. Gilardo Gomez	3. Ali Thani Juma
4. Zoran Vulic	4. Juergen Kohler	4. Luis Herrera	4. Ghanim Mubarek
5. Faruk Hadzibegic	5. Klaus Augenthaler	5. Leon Villa	5. Abdullah Ali Sultan
6. Davor Jozic	6. Guido Buchwald	6. Ricardo Perez	6. A. Mohamed Abdullah
7. Dragoljub Brnovic	7. Pierre Littbarski	7. Carlos Estrada	7. Fahd Khamees
8. Safet Susic	8. Thomas Haessler	8. Gabriel Gomez	8. Khalid Ismail Mubarak
9. Darko Pancev	9. Rudi Voeller	9. Miguel Paz	9. Abdul Aziz Mohamed
10. Dragan Stojkovic	10. Lothar Matthaeus	10. Carlos Valderrama	10. Adnan Al Talyani
11. Zlatko Vujovic	11. Frank Mill	11. Bernardo Redin	11. Zuhair Bakheet
12. Fahrudin Omerovic	12. Raimund Aumann	12. Eduardo Garcia	12. Ghuloum Abbas
13. Srecko Katanec	13. Karlheinz Riedle	13. Carlos Mario Hoyos	13. Hassan Mohamed
14. Alen Boksic	14. Thomas Berthold	14. Leonel Alvarez	14. Nasser K. Mubarak
15. Robert Prosinecki	15. Uwe Bein	15. Luis Carlos Perea	15. Ibrahim M. Abdulrahman
16. Refik Sabanadzovic	16. Paul Steiner	16. Arnolda Iguaran	16. Salim Mubarak
17. Robert Jarni	17. Andreas Moeller	17. Geovanis Cassiani	17. Mohsin Musabbah Faraj
18. Mirsad Baljic	18. Juergen Klinsmann	18. Wilmer Cabrera	18. Fahd Abdul Rahman
19. Dejan Savicevic	19. Hans Pfluegler	19. Freddy Rincon	19. Eissa M. Abdulrahman
20. Davor Suker	20. Olaf Thon	20. Luis Fajardo	20. Yousuf Mohamed
21. Andrej Panadic	21. Guenter Hermann	21. Alexis Mendoza	21. Abdul Rahman Haddad
22. Dragoje Lekovic	22. Andreas Koepke	22. Ruben Hernandez	22. Abdul Hassan

Group E · Venues: Verona / Udine

Belgium   Uruguay   Spain   South Korea

Winners Europe Group 7 **Winners South America Group 1** **Winners Europe Group 6** **Winners East & West Asia**

Belgium v Switzerland	1–0	Peru v Uruguay	0–2	Spain v Eire	2–0	S. Korea v Qatar	0–0
Czech. v Belgium	0–0	Bolivia v Uruguay	2–1	Spain v N. Ireland	4–0	S. Korea v N. Korea	1–0
Portugal v Belgium	1–1	Uruguay v Bolivia	2–0	Malta v Spain	0–2	China v S. Korea	0–1
Belgium v Czech.	2–1	Uruguay v Peru	2–0	N. Ireland v Spain	0–2	S. Arabia v S. Korea	0–2
Luxembourg v Belgium	0–5			Spain v Malta	4–0	UAE v S. Korea	2–0
Belgium v Portugal	3–0			Eire v Spain	1–0		
Switzerland v Belgium	2–2			Hungary v Spain	2–2		
Belgium v Luxembourg	1–1			Spain v Hungary	4–0		

Manager:	*Manager:*	*Manager:*	*Manager:*
Guy Thys	Oscar Tabarez	Luis Suarez	Lee Hoe-Taik
Squad:	*Squad:*	*Squad:*	*Squad:*
1. Michel Preud'Homme	1. Fernando Alvez	1. Andoni Zubizarreta	1. Kim Poong-joo
2. Eric Gerets	2. Nelson Gutierrez	2. Chendo	2. Park Kyung-joon
3. Philippe Albert	3. Hugo De Leon	3. Manuel Jiminez	3. Choi Kang-hee
4. Leo Clijsters	4. Jose Herrera	4. Genaro Andrinua	4. Yoon Deuk-yeo
5. Bruno Versavel	5. Jose Perdomo	5. Manuel Sanchis	5. Chung Yong-hwan
6. Marc Emmers	6. Alfonso Dominguez	6. Rafael Martin Vazquez	6. Lee Tae-ho
7. Stephane Demol	7. Antonio Alzamendi	7. Miguel Pardeza	7. Noh Soo-jin
8. Franky Van der Elst	8. Santiago Ostolaza	8. Enrique Sanchez	8. Chung Hae-won
9. Marc Degryse	9. Enzo Francescoli	9. Emilio Butragueno	9. Hwang Bo-kwan
10. Enzo Scifo	10. Ruben Paz	10. Fernando Gomez	10. Lee Sang-yoon
11. Jan Ceulemans	11. Ruben Sosa	11. Francisco Villaroya	11. Byun Byung-joo
12. Gilbert Bodart	12. Eduardo Pereira	12. Rafael Martinez	12. Lee Heung-sil
13. Georges Grun	13. Felipe Revelez	13. Juan Carlos Ablanedo	13. Chung Jong-soo
14. Nico Claesen	14. Jose Pintos-Saldanha	14. Alberto Gorriz	14. Choi Soon-ho
15. Jean-Francois De Sart	15. Carlos Correa	15. Roberto	15. Cho Min-kook
16. Michel De Wolf	16. Pablo Bengoechea	16. Jose Maria Baquero	16. Kim Joo-sung
17. Pascal Plovie	17. Sergio Martinez	17. Fernando Hierro	17. Gu Sang-bum
18. Lorenzo Staelens	18. Carlos Aguilera	18. Rafa Paz	18. Hwang Seon-hong
19. Marc Van der Linden	19. Daniel Fonseca	19. Julio Salinas	19. Jeong Gi-dong
20. Filip De Wilde	20. Ruben Pereira	20. Manolo	20. Hong Myung-bo
21. Marc Wilmots	21. William Castro	21. Michel	21. Choi In-young
22. Patrick Vervoort	22. Adolfo Zeoli	22. Jose Ochotorena	22. Lee Young-jin

Group F — Venues: Palermo / Cagliari

England
Runners-up Europe Group 2

England v Sweden	0–0
Albania v England	0–2
England v Albania	5–0
England v Poland	3–0
Sweden v England	0–0
Poland v England	0–0

Manager:
Bobby Robson
Squad:
1. Peter Shilton
2. Gary Stevens
3. Stuart Pearce
4. Neil Webb
5. Des Walker
6. Terry Butcher
7. Bryan Robson
8. Chris Waddle
9. Peter Beardsley
10. Gary Lineker
11. John Barnes
12. Paul Parker
13. Chris Woods
14. Mark Wright
15. Tony Dorigo
16. Steve McMahon
17. David Platt
18. Steve Hodge
19. Paul Gascoigne
20. Trevor Steven
21. Steve Bull
22. Dave Beasant

R. Ireland
Runners-up Europe Group 6

N. Ireland v R. Ireland	0–0
Spain v R. Ireland	2–0
Hungary v R. Ireland	0–0
R. Ireland v Spain	1–0
R. Ireland v Malta	2–0
R. Ireland v Hungary	2–0
R. Ireland v N. Ireland	3–0
Malta v R. Ireland	0–2

Manager:
Jack Charlton
Squad:
1. Pat Bonner
2. Chris Morris
3. Steve Staunton
4. Mick McCarthy
5. Kevin Moran
6. Ronnie Whelan
7. Paul McGrath
8. Ray Houghton
9. John Aldridge
10. Tony Cascarino
11. Kevin Sheedy
12. David O'Leary
13. Andy Townsend
14. Chris Hughton
15. Bernie Slaven
16. John Sheridan
17. Niall Quinn
18. Frank Stapleton
19. David Kelly
20. John Byrne
21. Alan McLoughlin
22. Gerry Peyton

Holland
Winners Europe Group 4

Holland v Wales	1–0
W. Germany v Holland	0–0
Holland v W. Germany	1–1
Finland v Holland	0–1
Wales v Holland	1–2
Holland v Finland	3–0

Manager:
Leo Beenhakker
Squad:
1. Hans van Breukelen
2. Berry van Aerle
3. Frank Rijkaard
4. Ronald Koeman
5. Andre van Tiggelen
6. Jan Wouters
7. Erwin Koeman
8. Gerald Vanenberg
9. Marco van Basten
10. Ruud Gullit
11. Richard Witschge
12. Wim Kieft
13. Graeme Rutjes
14. Johnny van't Schip
15. Bryan Roy
16. Joop Hiele
17. Hans Gillhaus
18. Henk Fraeser
19. John van Loen
20. Aron Winter
21. Danny Blind
22. Stanley Menzo

Egypt
Winners Africa Group B

Egypt v Liberia	2–0
Malawi v Egypt	1–1
Kenya v Egypt	0–0
Liberia v Egypt	1–0
Egypt v Malawi	1–0
Egypt v Kenya	2–0

Play-off

Algeria v Egypt	0–0
Egypt v Algeria	1–0

Manager:
Mahmoud El Gohary
Squad:
1. Ahmed Shoubeir
2. Ibrahim Hassan
3. Rabie Yassein
4. Hany Ramzy
5. Hesham Yakan
6. Ashraf Kasem
7. Ismail Youssef
8. Magdy Abdel-Ghani
9. Hossam Hassan
10. Gamal Abdel-Hamid
11. Tarek Soliman
12. Taher Abu Zeid
13. Ahmed Ramzy
14. Alaa Maihoub
15. Saber Eid
16. Magdy Tolba
17. Ayman Shawky
18. Osama Oraby
19. Abel Abdel-Rahman
20. Ahmed Abdou El-Kass
21. Ayman Taher
22. Thabet El-Battal

Group A

Italy	W	D	L	F	A	PTS
Italy	3	0	0	4	0	6
Czech.	2	0	1	6	3	4
Austria	1	0	2	2	3	2
USA	0	0	3	2	8	0

June 9, Rome [Att. 72,303]
Italy [0] 1   Austria [0] 0
ITALY: Zenga, Baresi, Bergomi, Ferri, Maldini, de Napoli, Donadoni, Ancelotti, Giannini, Vialli, Carnevale. Subs: de Agostini, Schillaci.
AUSTRIA: Lindenberger, Aigner, Russ, Pecl, Schoettel, Streiter, Artner, Linzmaier, Herzog, Ogris, Polster. Subs: Zsak, Hoertnagl.
Scorers: Schillaci for Italy.

June 10, Florence [Att. 33,266]
USA [0] 1   Czechoslovakia [2] 5
USA: Meola, Trittschuh, Windischmann, Harkes, Armstrong, Stollmeyer, Ramos, Murray, Caligiuri, Vermes, Wynalda.
CZECH.: Stejskal, Kadlec, Kocian, Straka, Chovanec, Hasek, Bilek, Kubik, Moravcik, Skuhravy, Knoflicek.
Scorers: Skuhravy 2, Bilek (pen.), Hasek, Luhovy (sub) for Czechoslovakia; Caligiuri for USA.

June 14, Rome [Att. 73,423]
Italy [1] 1   USA [0] 0
ITALY: Zenga, Baresi, Bergomi, Ferri, Maldini, de Napoli, Donadoni, Berti, Giannini, Vialli, Carnevale. Sub: Schillaci.
USA: Meola, Doyle, Windischmann, Harkes, Armstrong, Banks, Ramos, Balboa, Murray, Caligiuri, Vermes. Subs: Sullivan, Stollmeyer.
Scorers: Giannini for Italy.

June 15, Florence [Att. 38,962]
Austria [0] 0   Czechoslovakia [1] 1
AUSTRIA: Lindenberger, Aigner, Pfeffer, Russ, Pecl, Schoettel, Hoertnagl, Zsak, Herzog, Rodax, Polster. Subs: Streiter, Ogris.
CZECH.: Stejskal, Kadlec, Kocian, Nemecek, Chovanec, Hasek, Bilek, Kubik, Moravcik, Skuhravy, Knoflicek. Subs: Bielik, Weiss.
Scorers: Bilek (pen.) for Czechoslovakia.

June 19, Rome [Att. 73,303]
Italy [1] 2   Czechoslovakia [0] 0
ITALY: Zenga, Baresi, Bergomi, Ferri, Maldini, de Napoli, Donadoni, Berti, Giannini, Baggio, Schillaci. Subs: de Agostini, Vierchowod.
CZECH.: Stejskal, Kadlec, Kinier, Nemecek, Chovanec, Hasek, Bilek, Weiss, Moravcik, Skuhravy, Knoflicek. Subs: Bielik, Griga.
Scorers: Schillaci, Baggio for Italy.

June 19, Florence [Att. 34,857]
USA [0] 1   Austria [0] 2
USA: Meola, Doyle, Windischmann, Harkes, Armstrong, Banks, Ramos, Balboa, Murray, Caligiuri, Vermes. Subs: Wynalda, Bliss.
AUSTRIA: Lindenberger, Aigner, Streiter, Pfeffer, Pecl, Artner, Zsak, Ogris, Herzog, Rodax, Polster. Subs: Reisinger, Glatzmayer.
Scorers: Ogris, Rodax for Austria; Murray for USA.

Group B

Cameroon	W	D	L	F	A	PTS
Cameroon	2	0	1	3	5	4
Romania	1	1	1	4	3	3
Argentina	1	1	1	3	2	3
USSR	1	0	2	4	4	2

June 8, Milan [Att. 73,780]
Argentina [0] 0   Cameroon [0] 1
ARGENTINA: Pumpido, Ruggeri, Simon, Fabbri, Lorenzo, Batista, Burruchaga, Basualdo, Sensini, Balbo, Maradona. Subs: Caniggia, Calderon.
CAMEROON: N'kono, Ndip, Massing, Tataw, Kunde, Ebwelle, Mbouh, Kana Biyick, Mfede, Omam Biyick, Makanaky. Subs: Libiih, Milla.
Scorers: Omam Biyick for Cameroon.

June 9, Bari [Att. 42,907]
USSR [0] 0   Romania [1] 2
USSR: Dasayev, Kuznetsov, Khidiatullin, Gorlukovich, Aleinikov, Litovchenko, Bessonov, Zavarov, Rats, Protasov, Dobrovolski. Subs: Yeremchuk, Borodiuk.
ROMANIA: Lung, Rednic, Andone, Popescu, Klein, Lacatus, Sabau, Lupescu, Timofte, Rotariu, Raducioiu. Sub: Balint.
Scorers: Lacatus 2 (1 pen.) for Romania.

June 13, Naples [Att. 55,759]
Argentina [1] 2   USSR [0] 0
ARGENTINA: Pumpido, Serrizuela, Simon, Monzon, Troglio, Batista, Burruchaga, Basualdo, Olarticoechea, Caniggia, Maradona. Subs: Goycochea, Lorenzo.
USSR: Uvarov, Kuznetsov, Khidiatullin, Gorlukovich, Aleinikov, Zygmantovich, Bessonov, Shalimov, Zavarov, Protasov, Dobrovolski. Sub: Litovchenko.
Scorers: Troglio, Burruchaga for Argentina.

June 14, Bari [Att. 38,687]
Cameroon [0] 2   Romania [0] 1
CAMEROON: N'kono, Ndip, Onana, Tataw, Kunde, Ebwelle, Mbouh, Maboang, Mfede, Omam Biyick, Makanaky. Subs: Pagal, Milla.
ROMANIA: Lung, Rednic, Andone, Popescu, Klein, Lacatus, Sabau, Hagi, Timofte, Rotariu, Raducioiu. Subs: Balint, Dumitrescu.
Scorers: Milla 2 for Cameroon; Balint for Romania.

June 18, Naples [Att. 52,733]
Argentina [0] 1   Romania [0] 1
ARGENTINA: Goycochea, Serrizuela, Simon, Monzon, Troglio, Batista, Burruchaga, Basualdo, Olarticoechea, Caniggia, Maradona. Subs: Giusti, Dezotti.
ROMANIA: Lung, Rednic, Andone, Popescu, Klein, Lacatus, Sabau, Hagi, Lupescu, Rotariu, Balint. Subs: Lupu, Mateut.
Scorers: Monzon for Argentina; Balint for Romania.

June 18, Bari [Att. 37,307]
Cameroon [0] 0   USSR [2] 4
CAMEROON: N'kono, Ndip, K. Biyick, Onana, Tataw, Kunde, Ebwelle, Mbouh, Mfede, O. Biyick, Makanaky.
USSR: Uvarov, Kuznetsov, Khidiatullin, Gorlukovich, Aleinikov, Litovchenko, Demianenko, Zygmantovich, Shalimov, Protasov, Dobrovolski. Sub: Zavarov.
Scorers: Protasov, Zygmantovich, Zavarov, Dobrovolski for USSR.

Group C

Brazil	W	D	L	F	A	PTS
Brazil	3	0	0	4	1	6
Costa Rica	2	0	1	3	2	4
Scotland	1	0	2	2	3	2
Sweden	0	0	3	3	6	0

June 10, Turin [Att. 62,628]
Brazil [1] 2   Sweden [0] 1
BRAZIL: Taffarel, Galvao, Ricardo Gomez, Mozer, Jorginho, Valdo, Branco, Dunga, Alemao, Muller, Careca. Sub: Silas.
SWEDEN: Ravelli, Larsson, Ljung, R. Nilsson, Schwarz, Limpar, Thern, J. Nilsson, Ingesson, Brolin, Magnusson. Subs: Pettersson, Stroemberg.
Scorers: Careca 2 for Brazil; Brolin for Sweden.

June 11, Genoa [Att. 30,867]
Scotland [0] 0   Costa Rica [0] 1
SCOTLAND: Leighton, Gough, Malpas, McPherson, McLeish, Aitken, McStay, McCall, Bett, Johnston, McInally. Subs: McKimmie, McCoist.
COSTA RICA: Conejo, Flores, Montero, Marchena, Chavarria, Chavez, Gonzalez, Gomez, Ramirez, Cayasso, Jara. Sub: Medford.
Scorers: Cayasso for Costa Rica.

June 16, Turin [Att. 58,007]
Brazil [1] 1   Costa Rica [0] 0
BRAZIL: Taffarel, Galvao, Ricardo Gomez, Mozer, Jorginho, Valdo, Branco, Dunga, Alemao, Muller, Careca. Subs: Silas, Bebeto.
COSTA RICA: Conejo, Flores, Montero, Marchena, Chavarria, Chavez, Gonzalez, Gomez, Ramirez, Cayasso, Jara. Subs: Mayers, Guimaraes.
Scorers: Marchena o.g. for Brazil.

June 16, Genoa [Att. 31,823]
Scotland [1] 2   Sweden [0] 1
SCOT.: Leighton, Levein, Malpas, McPherson, McLeish, Aitken, MacLeod, McCall, Durie, Fleck, Johnston.
SWEDEN: Ravelli, Larsson, Hysen, R. Nilsson, Schwarz, Limpar, Thern, J. Nilsson, Ingesson, Brolin, Pettersson. Subs: Stroemberg, Ekstrom.
Scorers: McCall, Johnston (pen.) for Scotland; Stroemberg for Sweden.

June 20, Turin [Att. 62,502]
Brazil [0] 1   Scotland [0] 0
BRAZIL: Taffarel, Galvao, Ricardo Gomez, Ricardo Rocha, Jorginho, Valdo, Branco, Dunga, Alemao, Romario, Careca. Sub: Muller.
SCOTLAND: Leighton, McKimmie, Malpas, McPherson, McLeish, Aitken, McStay, MacLeod, McCall, McCoist, Johnston. Subs: Gillespie, Fleck.
Scorers: Muller for Brazil.

June 20, Genoa [Att. 30,223]
Sweden [1] 1   Costa Rica [0] 2
SWEDEN: Ravelli, Larsson, Hysen, R. Nilsson, Schwarz, J. Nilsson, Ingesson, Stroemberg, Brolin, Ekstrom, Pettersson. Subs: Gren, Engqvist.
COSTA RICA: Conejo, Flores, Montero, Marchena, Chavarria, Chavez, Gonzalez, Gomez, Ramirez, Cayasso, Jara. Subs: Medford, Guimaraes.
Scorers: Ekstrom for Swe.; Flores, Medford for C. Rica.

Group D

	W	D	L	F	A	PTS
W. Germany	2	1	0	10	3	5
Yugoslavia	2	0	1	6	5	4
Colombia	1	1	1	3	2	3
UAE	0	0	3	2	11	0

June 9, Bologna [Att. 30,791]
UAE [0] 0   Colombia [0] 2

U.A.E.: Faraj, E. Abdulrahman, I. Abdulrahman, Y. Mohamed, K.G. Mubarak, A. Abdullah, N. Mubarak, Abbas, Juma, F. Khamees, Al Talyani. Sub: Sultan.
COLOMBIA: Higuita, Herrera, Perea, Escobar, G. Gomez, Alvarez, G. Gomez, Valderrama, Redin, Iguaran, Rincon. Sub: Estrada
Scorers: Redin, Valderrama for Colombia.

June 10, Milan [Att. 74,765]
W. Germany [2] 4   Yugoslavia [0] 1

W. GERMANY: Illgner, Reuter, Brehme, Berthold, Augenthaler, Buchwald, Haessler, Matthaeus, Bein, Klinsmann, Voeller. Subs: Littbarski, Moeller.
YUGO.: Ivkovich, Spasic, Vulic, Hadzibegic, Jozic, Susic, Baljic, Stojkovic, Katanec, Vujovic, Savicevic.
Scorers: Matthaeus 2, Klinsmann, Voeller for W. Germany; Jozic for Yugoslavia.

June 14, Bologna [Att. 32,257]
Yugoslavia [0] 1   Colombia [0] 0

YUGO.: Ivkovich, Spasic, Stanojkovic, Hadzibegic, Jozic, Susic, Brnovic, Stojkovic, Katanec, Vujovic, Sabanadzovic. Subs: Jarni, Pancev.
COLOMBIA: Higuita, Herrera, Perea, Escobar, G. Gomez, Alvarez, G. Gomez, Valderrama, Redin, Iguaran, Rincon. Subs: Hernandez, Estrada.
Scorers: Jozic for Yugoslavia.

June 15, Milan [Att. 71,167]
W. Germany [2] 5   UAE [0] 1

W.G.: Illgner, Reuter, Brehme, Berthold, Augenthaler, Buchwald, Haessler, Matthaeus, Bein, Klinsmann, Voeller.
U.A.E.: Faraj, E. Abdulrahman, I. Abdulrahman, Y. Mohamed, K.G. Mubarak, A. Abdullah, N. Mubarak, Abbas, Juma, K.I. Mubarak, Al Talyani.
Scorers: Voeller 2, Klinsmann, Matthaeus, Bein for W. Germany; K.I. Mubarak for U.A.E.

June 19, Milan [Att. 72,510]
W. Germany [0] 1   Colombia [0] 1

W. GERMANY: Illgner, Reuter, Pfluegler, Berthold, Augenthaler, Buchwald, Haessler, Matthaeus, Bein, Klinsmann, Voeller. Subs: Littbarski, Thon.
COLOMBIA: Higuita, Herrera, Perea, Escobar, G. Gomez, Alvarez, G. Gomez, Valderrama, Estrada, Fajardo, Rincon.
Scorers: Littbarski for W. Ger.; Rincon for Colombia.

June 19, Bologna [Att. 27,833]
Yugoslavia [2] 4   UAE [1] 1

YUGOSLAVIA: Ivkovich, Spasic, Stanojkovic, Hadzibegic, Jozic, Susic, Brnovic, Stojkovic, Pancev, Vujovic, Sabanadzovic. Sub: Prosinecki, Vulic.
U.A.E.: Faraj, E. Abdulrahman, I. Abdulrahman, K.G. Mubarak, A. Abdullah, Al Haddad, N. Mubarak, Abbas, Juma, K.I. Mubarak, Al Talyani.
Scorers: Susic, Pancev 2, Prosinecki for Yugo; Juma for UAE.

Group E

	W	D	L	F	A	PTS
Spain	2	1	0	5	2	5
Belgium	2	0	1	6	3	4
Uruguay	1	1	1	2	3	3
S. Korea	0	0	3	1	6	0

June 12, Verona [Att. 32,486]
Belgium [0] 2   S. Korea [0] 0

BELGIUM: Preud'homme, Gerets, De Wolf, Demol, Clijsters, Emmers, Versavel, Van der Elst, Scifo, Van der Linden, Degryse. Sub: Ceulemans.
SOUTH KOREA: Choi In, Park, Choi Kang, Chung Yong, Hong, Gu, Choi Soon, Noh, Lee Young, Kim Joo, Hwang Bo. Subs: Lee Tae, Cho.
Scorers: Degryse, De Wolf for Belgium.

June 13, Udine [Att. 35,713]
Uruguay [0] 0   Spain [0] 0

URUGUAY: Alvez, Gutierrez, De Leon, Herrera, Perdomo, Dominguez, Pereira, Alzamendi, Paz, Francescoli, Sosa. Subs: Correa, Aguilera.
SPAIN: Zubizarreta, Chendo, Jiminez, Andrinua, Sanchis, Martin Vazquez, Roberto, Villaroya, Michel, Butragueno, Manolo. Subs: Gorriz, Rafa Paz.

June 17, Verona [Att. 33,759]
Belgium [2] 3   Uruguay [0] 1

BELG.: Preud'homme, Gerets, De Wolf, Demol, Clijsters, Grun, Versavel, Van der Elst, Scifo, Ceulemans, Degryse.
URUGUAY: Alvez, Gutierrez, De Leon, Herrera, Perdomo, Dominguez, Ostolaza, Alzamendi, Paz, Francescoli, Sosa. Subs: Aguilera, Bengoechea.
Scorers: Clijsters, Scifo, Ceulemans for Belgium; Bengoechea for Uruguay.

June 17, Udine [Att. 32,733]
S. Korea [1] 1   Spain [1] 3

SOUTH KOREA: Choi In, Park, Choi Kang, Yoon, Chung Hae, Hong, Gu, Choi Soon, Byun, Kim Joo, Hwang Bo. Subs: Noh, Chung Jong.
SPAIN: Zubizarreta, Chendo, Andrinua, Sanchis, Martin Vazquez, Roberto, Gorriz, Villaroya, Michel, Butragueno, Salinas. Subs: Gomez, Baquero.
Scorers: Michel 3 for Spain; Hwang Bo for S. Korea.

June 21, Verona [Att. 35,950]
Belgium [1] 1   Spain [2] 2

BELGIUM: Preud'homme, Albert, De Wolf, Demol, Staelens, Emmers, Vervoort, Van der Elst, Scifo, Ceulemans, Degryse. Subs: Plovie, Van der Linden.
SPAIN: Zubizarreta, Chendo, Andrinua, Sanchis, Martin Vazquez, Roberto, Gorriz, Villaroya, Michel, Butragueno, Salinas. Subs: Martinez, Pardeza.
Scorers: Michel (pen.), Gorriz for Sp.; Vervoort for Belg.

June 21, Udine [Att. 29,039]
S. Korea [0] 0   Uruguay [0] 1

SOUTH KOREA: Choi In, Park, Choi Kang, Chung Jong, Yoon, Hong, Lee Heung, Choi Soon, Byun, Kim Joo, Hwang Bo. Subs: Chung Hae, Hwang Seon.
URUGUAY: Alvez, Gutierrez, De Leon, Herrera, Perdomo, Dominguez, Ostolaza, Martinez, Paz, Francescoli, Sosa. Subs: Aguilera, Fonseca.
Scorers: Fonseca for Uruguay.

Group F

	W	D	L	F	A	PTS
England	1	2	0	2	1	4
Ireland	0	3	0	2	2	3
Holland	0	3	0	2	2	3
Egypt	0	2	1	1	2	2

June 11, Cagliari [Att. 35,238]
England [1] 1   R. of Ireland [0] 1

ENGLAND: Shilton, Stevens, Pearce, Walker, Butcher, Robson, Gascoigne, Barnes, Beardsley, Lineker, Waddle. Subs: McMahon, Bull.
IRELAND: Bonner, Morris, Staunton, McCarthy, Moran, McGrath, Townsend, Houghton, Sheedy, Cascarino, Aldridge. Sub: McLoughlin.
Scorers: Lineker for England; Sheedy for R. of Ireland.

June 12, Palermo [Att. 33,288]
Holland [0] 1   Egypt [0] 1

HOLLAND: van Breukelen, van Aerle, van Tiggelen, R. Koeman, Rutjes, Rijkaard, Wouters, E. Koeman, Vanenberg, Gullit, van Basten. Subs: Kieft, Witschge.
EGYPT: Shoubeir, Yassein, H. Ramzy, Yakan, I. Hassan, Youssef, Abdel-Ghani, Abdel-Hamid, El Kass, A. Ramzy, H. Hassan. Subs: Tolba, Abdel-Rahman.
Scorers: Kieft for Holland; Abdel-Ghani (pen.) for Egypt.

June 16, Cagliari [Att. 35,267]
England [0] 0   Holland [0] 0

ENGLAND: Shilton, Parker, Pearce, Walker, Butcher, Wright, Gascoigne, Robson, Barnes, Lineker, Waddle. Subs: Bull, Platt.
HOLLAND: van Breukelen, van Aerle, van Tiggelen, R. Koeman, van't Schip, Rijkaard, Wouters, Gillhaus, Witschge, Gullit, van Basten. Sub: Kieft.

June 17, Palermo [Att. 33,288]
R. of Ireland [0] 0   Egypt [0] 0

IRELAND: Bonner, Morris, Staunton, McCarthy, Moran, McGrath, Townsend, Houghton, Sheedy, Cascarino, Aldridge. Subs: McLoughlin, Quinn.
EGYPT: Shoubeir, Yassein, H. Ramzy, Yakan, I. Hassan, Youssef, Tolba, Abdel-Ghani, Oraby, El Kass, H. Hassan. Subs: Abdel-Hamid, Abu Zeid.

June 21, Cagliari [Att. 34,959]
England [0] 1   Egypt [0] 0

ENGLAND: Shilton, Parker, Pearce, Walker, Wright, Gascoigne, McMahon, Barnes, Lineker, Bull, Waddle. Subs: Beardsley, Platt.
EGYPT: Shoubeir, Yassein, H. Ramzy, Yakan, I. Hassan, Youssef, Abdel-Hamid, Abdel-Ghani, A. Ramzy, El Kass, H. Hassan. Subs: Abdel-Rahman, Soliman.
Scorers: Wright for England.

June 21, Palermo [Att. 33,288]
R. of Ireland [0] 1   Holland [1] 1

IRELAND: Bonner, Morris, Staunton, McCarthy, Moran, McGrath, Townsend, Houghton, Sheedy, Quinn, Aldridge. Subs: Whelan, Cascarino.
HOLLAND: van Breukelen, van Aerle, van Tiggelen, R. Koeman, Rijkaard, Wouters, Gillhaus, Witschge, Kieft, Gullit, van Basten. Subs: Fraeser, van Loen.
Scorers: Gullit for Holland; Quinn for R. of Ireland.

Second Phase

June 23, Naples [Att. 50,026]
Cameroon [0] 2   Colombia [0] 1
(aet, 90 mins 0-0)

CAMEROON: N'kono, Ndip, Kana Biyick, Onana, Tataw, Ebwelle, Mbouh, Maboang, Mfede, Omam Biyick, Makanaky. Subs: Milla, Djonkep.
COLOMBIA: Higuita, Herrera, Perea, Escobar, Gilardo Gomez, Alvarez, Gabriel Gomez, Valderrama, Estrada, Fajardo, Rincon. Subs: Iguaran, Redin.
Scorers: Milla 2 for Cameroon; Redin for Colombia.

June 23, Bari [Att. 47,673]
Czechoslovakia [1] 4   Costa Rica [0] 1

CZECHOSLOVAKIA: Stejskal, Kadlec, Kocian, Straka, Chovanec, Hasek, Bilek, Moravcik, Kubik, Skuhravy, Knoflicek.
COSTA RICA: Barrantes, Flores, Montero, Marchena, Chavarria, Chavez, Gonzalez, Obando, Ramirez, Cayasso, Jara. Subs: Medford, Guimaraes.
Scorers: Skuhravy 3, Kubik for Czechoslovakia; Gonzalez for Costa Rica.

June 24, Turin [Att. 61,381]
Brazil [0] 0   Argentina [0] 1

BRAZIL: Claudio Taffarel, Mauro Galvao, Ricardo Gomez, Ricardo Rocha, Jorginho, Valdo, Branco, Dunga, Alemao, Muller, Careca. Subs: Silas, Renato.
ARGENTINA: Goycochea, Giusti, Simon, Ruggeri, Monzon, Troglio, Burruchaga, Basauldo, Olarticoechea, Caniggia, Maradona. Sub: Calderon.
Scorers: Caniggia for Argentina.

June 24, Milan [Att. 74,559]
West Germany [0] 2   Holland [0] 1

W. GERMANY: Illgner, Reuter, Brehme, Berthold, Augenthaler, Buchwald, Kohler, Matthaeus, Littbarski, Klinsmann, Voeller. Sub: Riedle.
HOLLAND: van Breukelen, van Aerle, van Tiggelen, R. Koeman, Rijkaard, Wouters, van't Schip, Winter, Witschge, Gullit, van Basten. Subs: Kieft, Gillhaus.
Scorers: Klinsmann, Brehme for West Germany; R. Koeman (pen.) for Holland.

June 25, Genoa [Att. 31,818]
Rep. of Ireland [0] 0   Romania [0] 0
(aet, 90 mins 0-0, Rep of Ireland won 5-4 on penalties)

REPUBLIC OF IRELAND: Bonner, Morris, Staunton, McCarthy, Moran, McGrath, Townsend, Houghton, Sheedy, Quinn, Aldridge. Subs: Cascarino, O'Leary.
ROMANIA: Lung, Rednic, Andone, Popescu, Klein, Sabau, Hagi, Lupescu, Rotariu, Raducioiu, Balint. Subs: Lupu, Timofte.

June 25, Rome [Att. 73,303]
Italy [0] 2   Uruguay [0] 0

ITALY: Zenga, Baresi, Bergomi, Ferri, Maldini, de Napoli, de Agostini, Berti, Giannini, Baggio, Schillaci. Subs: Serena, Vierchowod.
URUGUAY: Alvez, Pintos-Saldanha, Gutierrez, De Leon, Perdomo, Dominguez, Ruben Pereira, Ostolaza, Aguilera, Francescoli, Fonseca. Subs: Sosa, Alzamendi.
Scorers: Schillaci, Serena for Italy.

June 26, Verona [Att. 35,500]
Spain [0] 1   Yugoslavia [0] 2
(aet, 90 mins 1-1)

SPAIN: Zubizarreta, Chendo, Andrinua, Sanchis, Martin Vazquez, Roberto, Gorriz, Villaroya, Michel, Butragueno, Salinas. Subs: Jiminez, Rafa Paz.
YUGOSLAVIA: Ivkovich, Spasic, Katanec, Hadzibegic, Jozic, Susic, Brnovic, Stojkovic, Pancev, Vujovic, Sabanadzovic. Subs: Savicevic, Vulic.
Scorers: Stojkovic 2 for Yugoslavia; Salinas for Spain.

June 26, Bologna [Att. 34,520]
England [0] 1   Belgium [0] 0
(aet, 90 mins 0-0)

ENGLAND: Shilton, Parker, Pearce, Walker, Butcher, Wright, Gascoigne, McMahon, Barnes, Lineker, Waddle. Subs: Platt, Bull.
BELGIUM: Preud'homme, Gerets, De Wolf, Clijsters, Demol, Versavel, Grun, Van der Elst, Scifo, Ceulemans, Degryse. Subs: Claesen, Vervoort.
Scorers: Platt for England.

Quarter-Finals

June 30, Florence [Att. 38,971]
Argentina [0] 0 Yugoslavia [0] 0

(aet, 90 mins 0-0, Argentina won 3-2 on penalties)
ARGENTINA: Goycochea, Giusti, Simon, Ruggeri, Serrizuela, Calderon, Burruchaga, Basualdo, Olarticoechea, Caniggia, Maradona. Subs: Troglio, Dezotti.
YUGOSLAVIA: Ivkovich, Spasic, Hadzibegic, Jozic, Susic, Brnovic, Stojkovic, Vulic, Prosinecki, Vujovic, Sabanadzovic. Sub: Savicevic, Jarni.

July 1, Milan [Att. 73,347]
Czech. [0] 0 W. Germany [1] 1

CZECHOSLOVAKIA: Stejskal, Kadlec, Kocian, Straka, Chovanec, Hasek, Bilek, Moravcik, Kubik, Skuhravy, Knoflicek. Subs: Nemecek, Griga.
WEST GERMANY: Illgner, Brehme, Berthold, Augenthaler, Buchwald, Kohler, Matthaeus, Bein, Littbarski, Klinsmann, Riedle. Sub: Moeller.
Scorers: Matthaeus (pen.) for West Germany.

June 30, Rome [Att. 73,303]
Italy [1] 1 Rep. of Ireland [0] 0

ITALY: Zenga, Baresi, Bergomi, Ferri, Maldini, de Napoli, de Agostini, Donadoni, Giannini, Baggio, Schillaci. Subs: Ancelotti, Serena.
REPUBLIC OF IRELAND: Bonner, Morris, Staunton, McCarthy, Moran, McGrath, Townsend, Houghton, Sheedy, Quinn, Aldridge. Subs: Cascarino, Sheridan.
Scorers: Schillaci for Italy.

July 1, Naples [Att. 55,205]
England [1] 3 Cameroon [0] 2
(aet, 90 mins 2-2)

ENGLAND: Shilton, Parker, Pearce, Walker, Butcher, Wright, Gascoigne, Platt, Barnes, Lineker, Waddle. Subs: Beardsley, Steven.
CAMEROON: N'kono, Kunde, Massing, Tataw, Ebwelle, Maboang, Libiih, Pagal, Mfede, O. Biyick, Makanaky. Subs: Milla, Ekeke.
Scorers: Platt, Lineker (2 pens.) for England; Kunde (pen.), Ekeke for Cameroon.

Semi-Finals

July 3, Naples [Att. 59,978]
Argentina [0] 1 Italy [1] 1

(aet, 90 mins 1-1, Argentina won 4-3 on penalties)

ARGENTINA: Goycochea, Giusti, Simon, Ruggeri, Serrizuela, Calderon, Burruchaga, Basualdo, Olarticoechea, Caniggia, Maradona. Subs: Troglio, Batista.
ITALY: Zenga, Baresi, Bergomi, Ferri, Maldini, de Napoli, de Agostini, Donadoni, Giannini, Vialli, Schillaci. Subs: Serena, Baggio.
Scorers: Schillaci for Italy; Caniggia for Argentina.

July 4, Florence [Att. 62,628]
W. Germany [0] 1 England [0] 1

(aet, 90 mins 1-1, West Germany won 4-3 on penalties)

WEST GERMANY: Illgner, Brehme, Berthold, Augenthaler, Buchwald, Kohler, Matthaeus, Thon, Haessler, Klinsmann, Voeller. Subs: Riedle, Reuter.
ENGLAND: Shilton, Parker, Pearce, Walker, Butcher, Wright, Gascoigne, Platt, Beardsley, Lineker, Waddle. Sub: Steven.
Scorers: Brehme for W. Ger.; Lineker for England.

Third Place Play-off

England [0] 1
Platt, 80

Italy [0] 2
Baggio, 70
Schillaci (pen.), 84

ENGLAND
1. Shilton (cap.)
2. Stevens
12. Parker
15. Dorigo
5. Walker
14. Wright
20. Steven
16. McMahon
17. Platt
9. Beardsley
10. Lineker
Subs:
8. Waddle (for Wright)
4. Webb (for McMahon)

ITALY
1. Zenga
3. Bergomi (cap.)
7. Maldini
2. Baresi
8. Vierchowod
5. Ferrara
4. de Agostini
9. Ancelotti
13. Giannini
15. Baggio
19. Schillaci
Subs:
10. Berti (for Giannini)
6. Ferri (for de Agostini)

Date: July 7th, 1990
Venue: Bari
Attendance: 51,426
Referee: Joel Quiniou (France)

The Final

Argentina [0] 0

West Germany [0] 1
Brehme (pen.), 85

ARGENTINA
12. Goycochea
19. Ruggeri
20. Simon
18. Serrizuela
 4. Basualdo
13. Lorenzo
21. Troglio
 7. Burruchaga
17. Sensini
10. Maradona (cap.)
 9. Dezotti
Subs:
15. Monzon (for Ruggeri)
 6. Calderon (for Burruchaga)

WEST GERMANY
 1. Illgner
14. Berthold
 3. Brehme
 4. Kohler
 5. Augenthaler
 6. Buchwald
 8. Haessler
10. Matthaeus (cap.)
 7. Littbarski
 9. Voeller
18. Klinsmann
Sub:
2 .Reuter (for Berthold)

Sendings off: Monzon (Arg.), Dezotti (Arg.).Bookings: Troglio (Arg.), Maradona (Arg), Voeller (W. Ger.).

Date: July 8th, 1990
Venue: Rome
Attendance: 73,603
Referee: Edgardo Codesal Mendez (Mexico)

World Cup '90: The goals

Total goals scored

There were a total of 115 goals scored in 52 matches at an average 2.21 per game. This is the lowest ever goals per game average for a World Cup tournament. The previous lowest average was 2.54 per game in Mexico in the 1986 finals when 132 goals were scored in 52 matches. The highest goals average was 5.38 in the 1954 finals when 140 goals were netted in 26 games.

When Andreas Brehme scored West Germany's World Cup winner from the penalty spot against Argentina it was the 1,443rd goal in World Cup finals history and it came in the 464th game.

The goalscorers

Salvatore Schillaci became the tournament's top marksman when he scored the match-winning goal from the penalty spot in the third-place play-off against England. It was his sixth goal of the finals. Just Fontaine, of France, remains the highest individual scorer in a World Cup finals tournament. The Morroccan-born striker netted 13 goals in the 1958 finals to shoot France into third place.

The highest aggregate goals total is 14, set by West Germany's Gerd Muller, who netted 10 goals in 1970 and four in 1974. Muller scored 19 goals in the 1970 competition, including the qualifying matches.

Gary Lineker holds the British record for most goals in aggregate in World Cup finals. He was the tournament's leading marksman in 1986 with six goals, and added another four during World Cup '90 not counting his successful spot-kick in the penalty shoot-out against West Germany in the semi-final.

Salvatore "Toto" Schillaci, the leading marksman in World Cup '90 with six goals

These were the men who found the back of the net during World Cup '90 (the totals do not include goals scored during penalty shoot-outs):

6: Schillaci (Italy).

5: Skuhravy (Czechoslovakia).

4: Lineker (England), Matthaeus (West Germany), Michel (Spain), Milla (Cameroon).

3: Brehme (West Germany), Klinsmann (West Germany), Platt (England), Voeller (West Germany).

127

World Cup '90: The final count

2: Baggio (Italy), Balint (Romania), Bilek (Czechoslovakia), Caniggia (Argentina), Careca (Brazil), Jozic (Yugoslavia), Lacatus (Romania), Muller (Brazil), Pancev (Yugoslavia), Redin (Colombia), Stojkovic (Yugoslavia)

1: Abdel-Ghani (Egypt), Ali Thani Juma (UAE), Bein (West Germany), Bengoechea (Argentina), O. Biyick (Cameroon), Brolin (Sweden), Burruchaga (Argentina), Caligiuri (USA), Cayasso (Costa Rica), Ceulemans (Belgium), Clijsters (Belgium), Degryse (Belgium), de Wolf (Belgium), Dobrovolski (USSR), Ekeke (Cameroon), Ekstroem (Sweden), Flores (Costa Rica), Fonseca (Uruguay), Giannini (Italy), Gonzalez (Costa Rica), Gorriz (Spain), Gullit (Holland), Hasek (Czechoslovakia), Kwan Hwang-Bo (South Korea), Johnston (Scotland), Kieft (Holland), R. Koeman (Holland), Kubik (Czechoslovakia), Kunde (Cameroon), Littbarski (West Germany), Luhovy (Czechoslovakia), McCall (Scotland), Medford (Costa Rica), Monzon (Argentina), K.I. Mubarak (UAE), Murray (USA), Ogris (Austria), Prosinecki (Yugoslavia), Protasov (USSR), Quinn (Rep. of Ireland), Rincon (Colombia), Rodax (Austria), Scifo (Belgium), Salinas (Spain), Serena (Italy), Sheedy (Rep. of Ireland), Stroemberg (Sweden), Susic (Yugoslavia), Troglio (Argentina), Valderrama (Colombia), Vervoort (Belgium), Wright (England), Zavarov (USSR), Zygmantovich (USSR).

Fastest goal

Safet Susic, Yugoslavian midfield veteran, scored the fastest goal of World Cup '90 when he netted against the United Arab Emirates after 3 mins 58 secs on June 19 in the Group D match in Bologna. The fastest goal in World Cup history was netted in 27 seconds by Manchester United's Bryan Robson for England against France in the 1982 finals in Spain.

Latest goal

David Platt's dramatic winner for England against Belgium in the second phase match in Bologna came in the 119th minute.

Bookings and sendings-off

There were a record 16 players sent off during World Cup '90, and another reecord 170 booked at an average 3.27 per game. The players ordered off:

Kana Biyick (Cameroon v Argentina); Massing (Cameroon v Argentina); Wynalda (USA v Czechoslovakia); Bessonov (USSR v Argentina; K.G. Mubarak (UAE v Yugoslavia); Artner (Austria v USA); Yoon Deuk-yeo (South Korea v Uruguay); R. Gomez (Brazil v Argentina); Rijkaard (Holland v West Germany); Voeller (West Germany v Holland); Sabanadzovic (Yugoslavia v Argentina); Moravcik (Czechoslovakia v West Germany); Giusti (Argentina v Italy); Monzon (Argentina v West Germany); Dezotti (Argentina v West Germany).

The crowds

Largest: 74,765 for West Germany v Yugoslavia, Milan, June 17. Smallest: 27,833 for Yugoslavia v UAE, Bologna, June 19. The record crowd for a World Cup tie remains the 205,000 (199,854 paid) that gathered for the decisive match in the 1950 finals between Brazil and Uruguay in Rio.

The receipts

A record £3,812,589 was taken for the World Cup final between West Germany and Argentina in Rome's Olympic Stadium on July 8. The attendance for the Final was 73,603.